60 years of Talyllyn Railway Volunteering

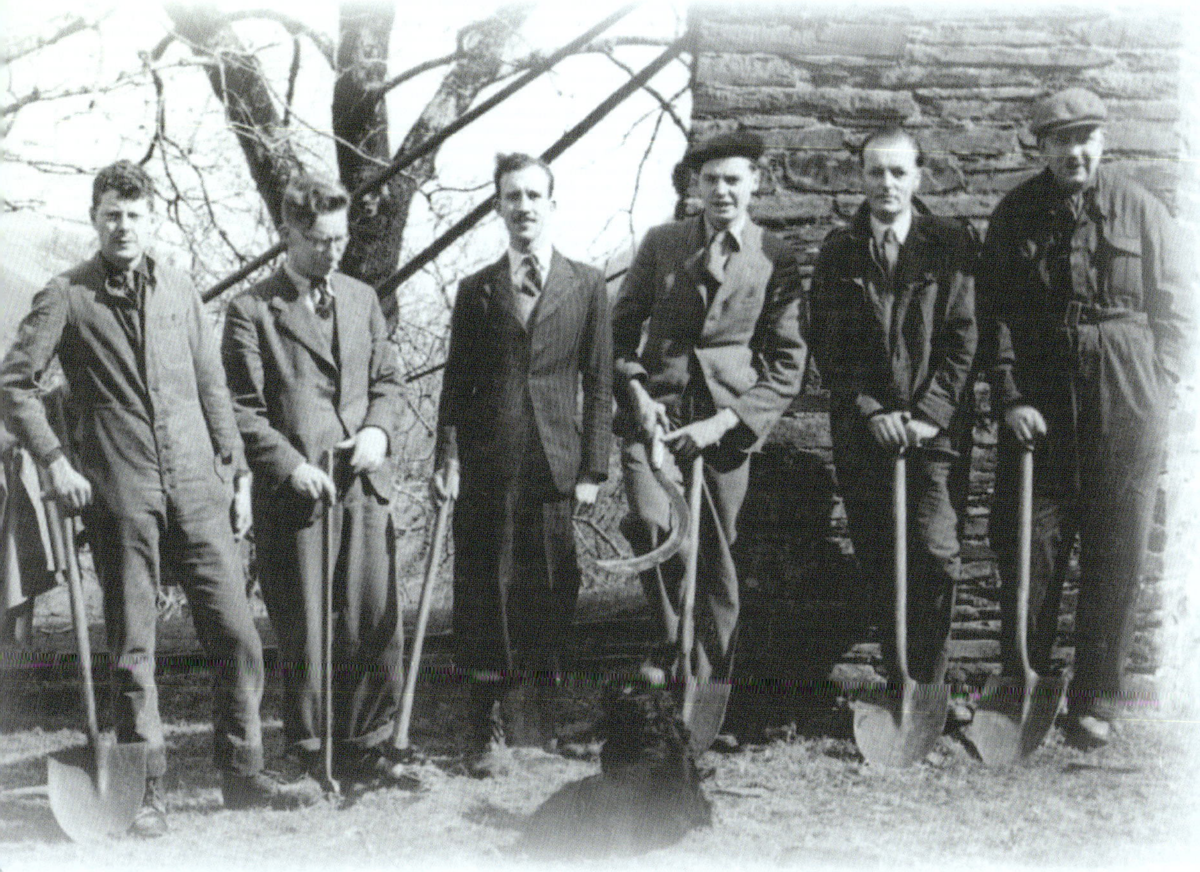

1951 - 2011

60 Years of Talyllyn Railway Volunteering

TALYLLYN preservation 60
1951 - 2011

Nigel Adams & Lawrence Garvey

© Talyllyn Railway Company 2011

ISBN 978 1 85794 369 6

All rights reserved. No part of this publication may be reproduced, stored in a retrieval system or transmitted, in any form or by any means, electronic, mechanical, photocopying, recording or otherwise, without prior permission in writing from Silver Link Publishing Ltd.

Silver Link Publishing Ltd
The Trundle
Ringstead Road
Great Addington
Kettering
Northants NN14 4BW

First published in 2011

Tel/Fax: 01536 330588
email: sales@nostalgiacollection.com
Website: www.nostalgiacollection.com

British Library Cataloguing in Publication Data

A catalogue record for this book is available from the British Library.

Printed and bound in the Czech Republic

DEDICATION

To the original members of the Talyllyn Railway Preservation Society, who had the foresight to form the Society and the belief that they could save the Talyllyn Railway from extinction.
To all who have volunteered, in whatever capacity, over the past 60 years to keep the TR running and make it what it is today.
To those volunteers, of whatever age, who have joined recently and who will be the lifeblood of the TRPS in the years to come.
To the 'volunteer grass widows and widowers' who support the TR by not complaining when their partners spend hours volunteering.

Authors' note

We are sure readers will appreciate that 29 people have written contributions for this book. Some of them volunteered a long time ago and have now ceased, some have been volunteering for a long time and are still active, and some are relatively new volunteers and have many years in front of them.

All of them have had to rely on their memories in writing their contributions, so it is inevitable that there will be some minor factual inconsistencies. Likewise there may be some small inconsistencies over terminology, and the use or otherwise of initial capital letters for certain grades.

We feel these are minor and do not detract from what is at the heart of this book – a fantastic record of 60 years of volunteering on the Talyllyn Railway. We hope you agree.

We feel very privileged to have been able to compile this book from the contributions.

Nigel Adams
Lawrence Garvey

CONTENTS

Introduction	7
1 Volunteers' stories	9
2 Volunteers photo gallery	101
3 Landmarks and events	112
Index	128

ACKNOWLEDGEMENTS

We feel a 'bit of a fraud' having our names on this book as the authors! It would be much more factual to describe us as the compilers.

Nigel had the idea and involved Lawrence, who is the TR Volunteer Coordinator, from the outset. We asked volunteers to write contributions and Lawrence used his computer skills to put them together. Because there is a finite number of words in any book, some of the contributions had to be edited and we hope that in doing so we have not upset anyone, but we did warn contributors from the start that this was always a possibility. Nigel chose most of the photographs from the TR Collection and some more from those submitted by contributors.

We are extremely grateful to the photographers whose pictures we have used. The TR Collection comprises photographs that have been given to the railway by those who took them, for the railway to use. Without the generosity of those photographers, compiling this book would have been much more difficult.

We owe a debt of gratitude to Lawrie Bowles and Roger Whitehouse who helped us by proofreading, although it has to be said that if there are any errors in the book we take full responsibility!

All who have contributed in any way to this book have done so for the benefit of the Talyllyn Railway, to which all royalties are being donated. We hope that many copies of this book will be sold so that the railway, to which we willingly give so much of our time, will be there for future generations to enjoy.

We also hope that the book will encourage more people to volunteer to work on the TR, as, without volunteers, it cannot be run! Over the years many people have thoroughly enjoyed volunteering, and we can assure anyone thinking of 'taking the plunge' and offering their services that they are assured of a warm welcome and will not regret it! Above all, they will enjoy themselves and make new friends, and we hope that the contributions in this book make that obvious.

Nigel Adams
Lawrence Garvey

THE TALYLLYN RAILWAY

INTRODUCTION

The Talyllyn Railway was the first preserved railway in the world. It was saved by the efforts of the early members of the Talyllyn Railway Preservation Society, which was formed at a meeting in Birmingham in October 1950, and the first train under Society auspices ran from Wharf station to Rhydyronen and back on 14 May 1951. Through the dedication and hard work of volunteers from all walks of life the TR was put back into running order, and in 1976 the extension to Nant Gwernol was opened. In 2005, HRH Prince Charles and the Duchess of Cornwall opened a completely rebuilt Wharf station complex. This cost £1.5 million, which was raised by the TRPS, with about 25% of the total coming from members and their efforts – a fantastic achievement.

In terms of passengers carried, the halcyon days of the TR were in the 1970s, when more than 100,000 passengers a year were carried. However, changing holiday patterns and cheaper foreign holidays have had a major effect on the number of people holidaying in the area, and now the TR carries about 45,000 passengers a year, which is still no mean achievement.

In a way, the TR has suffered by being the first preserved railway in the world because many other railways are now preserved and people have a lot more choice of locations – often much nearer to where they live. Nevertheless, the TR is still flourishing and nothing can take away from it the uniqueness of being the first preserved steam railway in the world, and one that is still running 60 years later and is mainly operated by volunteers.

There have been many words written about the TR over the last 60 years, but as far as we know this is the first book to concentrate on the stories of volunteers. We felt it would be good to do this to mark their huge contribution.

Our volunteers come from all walks of life and from all parts of the UK and the world. Some travel from America, Canada and Holland, to name but three countries. They undertake a wide variety of tasks, ranging from operating the railway to working on the outdoor gang, working in the Works, helping staff the TRPS stand at shows and exhibitions, and making things (such as flags) at home. The opportunities are endless and full training is given. Volunteers range in age from 14 to senior citizens. We also have the 'Tracksiders', who are under 14 and work under the supervision of adults (usually, but not always, their parents); when they reach the age of 14 they progress to being volunteers in their own right. Volunteering on the TR also gives you a wide circle of friends and acquaintances who share an interest.

Without in any way wishing to introduce party politics into this book, the present government is very keen on people taking an interest in their own community by volunteering to help run and organise things. This idea has been dubbed the 'Big Society'. TRPS members have been doing this very successfully for 60 years!

In this 60th anniversary year, the TRPS has a lot to celebrate, but above all this book is an attempt to celebrate and recognise the fantastic input by all the volunteers – past and present – who have made their contributions, whether large or small, to the successful operation of the Talyllyn Railway. It is a marvellous achievement.

We hope that by reading these stories others will be encouraged to offer their services to ensure that the Talyllyn Railway runs for future generations to enjoy.

Nigel Adams

1 Volunteers' stories

Alan Holmes

After such a long period of time, I could have chosen any one of the decades since 1950 to describe what I have been doing on the railway, but instead I would like to say something about my experience in the decade 2001-11, which I think is relevant.

It was during an Outdoor Week under the leadership of the 'Brutal Quarry Master' in 2003 that I reached the 50th

Volunteers' stories

anniversary of my first volunteer weekend on the railway and, coincidentally, my 70th birthday. I arranged for a special evening train to run up to Abergynolwyn where the catering department provided an excellent buffet, with wine and a barrel of beer. This was a year or two before old age and infirmity brought my active volunteering career – hefting jarrah sleepers, shovelling ballast and suchlike – to an end.

So we all settled down to enjoy a pint or two and nibbles when I realised that certain folk, the then Managing Director among them, were standing together and muttering 'wouldn't it be nice to have a history of the Society to stand alongside the Chief Engineer's book about his life as the 'Lord of Pendre Works' and so on. Someone turned to me and said, 'Not many people are here from the early days when the TRPS was formed – and soon there won't be any of them left.' Thanks for that, thought I!

The MD turned to me. 'Would you consider writing a book to cover the history of the Society's activities since the early days?'

Gulp! 'But I am neither a historian nor a man of letters,' said I.

'But you have written a book before (referring to my modest history of Bryneglwys slate quarry), so do think about it.'

I had another beer. They had already lined up a publisher, Rail Romances, which had produced the Chief Engineer's tome and was willing to consider doing another about the railway. That was a big bonus for me, so after a pause I said I would think about it.

When I did agree to go ahead with the project I was allowed free access to the company's records. There were many paper records to search, correspondence files, minute books, company reports and much legal material to work through. I put an appeal in the *Talyllyn News* for people's reminiscences of their volunteering work in past years and received many very valuable letters, which helped to fill in the early years in particular. I also used some tape-recorded conversations with now deceased officials, and others from the Museum archives.

During my long stint as a volunteer there were some duties I hadn't done, so the Traffic Manager of the day enrolled me as a (rather elderly) trainee so that I could get hands-on experience of operational matters. This was quite different from my earliest brief experience of guard duty – one day in the in summer 1958 I arrived at Wharf to be greeted by the then General Manager, who said, 'Alan, I'm glad you're here, we are short of guards today. Will you take this train out, please?' He handed me a cashbox, a whistle and gave me a very brief explanation of closing ticket numbers. 'Good luck!' and off we went up the line.

I was soon to discover that they did things differently in 2005, thank goodness. I was very impressed to be given a computer printout of my daily rosters with dates and reporting times all clearly written. I was lucky enough to win a footplate ride on *Dolgoch* one day, but this is no way of learning what is entailed in locomotive work, so in my manuscript I had to rely on conversations and the descriptions by some correspondents who gave me graphic details of the trips they had done, including some that were anything but smooth routine.

One task facing the author of any book is choosing a title. Tom Rolt, of course, got it dead right with his book *Railway Adventure*. I tossed around several suggestions to get something new, eventually coming up with *Talyllyn Revived: The story of the world's first Railway Preservation Society*. A bit cumbersome, I fear, but I wanted to get across the fact that it really was about a world first. Meanwhile I was gradually drafting my manuscript and submitting disks to the publisher. When I was getting along nicely, as I thought, I had a message to say that he had suffered a heart attack. Some months later he had a relapse and on medical advice he had to cut down drastically on his workload. He wrote to say how sorry he was but he could not proceed with my project.

I carried on until I felt it was complete, then submitted the manuscript to the MD who had asked me to embark on the book. 'Here you are, I've done what you asked me to do.'

There remained one further step to be made, choosing photographs and drawings to illustrate the story. Over the course of 60 years the railway has accumulated an enormous collection of photographs with no comprehensive catalogue, and nor are they all in one place. I trailed through many albums and boxes, slides and folders and holiday snaps, colour and monochrome, including some of my own, until I was going dizzy. Colour pictures are considerably more expensive to print than mono, which had to borne in mind in order to keep production costs to a reasonable level.

After several unsuccessful attempts to find a publisher, the TRPS Council approved the principle that the Talyllyn Railway would publish the book itself, which probably caused the Treasurer some misgivings over the cost. I kept a low profile while this was going on! A quote was accepted from a designer in the Isle of Wight, which involved several visits to their HQ. It was to be case-bound, of the same size and general outward appearance as the Chief Engineer's tome already mentioned, and would have a generous number of photographs taken over the previous half-century, including some in colour.

The designer in turn recommended a printer in Cheshire. The next step was to obtain a set of proofs and, while anxious to see them myself, I was persuaded, quite rightly, that an independent member of the railway hierarchy should do the proofreading; the Society's President kindly agreed to do this. It was hoped to make the book ready for Christmas 2009, but there were gremlins present that spoiled that plan. There were omissions in the text, some photos were fogged, and others appeared in the wrong place, but fortunately the printer admitted that the consignment was faulty. They agreed to rectify their mistakes and the Railway Shop was eventually supplied with a corrected stock, which you can see on the shelf today. Any mistakes now are mine!

I do not claim that my book is unique, and it is certainly not the first to chronicle the story of the first successful attempt by a voluntary body to take over a statutory public railway company and run it by largely volunteer labour. First and foremost are the book *Railway Adventure* by Tom Rolt and the film *Railway with a Heart of Gold* by the American film-maker Carson Davidson, now available on DVD. Both recall the early struggles and triumphs in the 1950s and they are real classics of their kind.

I am sure that there is probably a young member in the Society now who will live to chronicle the events on the TR in the next 50 years, starting perhaps with the Diamond Jubilee in May 2011. I shall not be there in 50 years time, but I am sure it will be a success story and I wish him or her well.

Chris White

It was with a slight shock that realisation dawned on me that, like many others, I have now been a Talyllyn volunteer in seven different decades. In every year since 1956 I have made some input to the total effort. This has been on several fronts: as a traffic volunteer; as writer, speaker and photographer; as working party

Chris White in June 1993. *R. J. Morland*

Volunteers' stories

organiser; on committees and in administration; on work for the museum; and in the local area group. The balance between these activities has varied over the years and has always been balanced against family commitments, a busy professional life and other interests.

My first experience of narrow gauge railways was on a visit to Wales to explore what remained – the Penrhyn main line, the Welshpool & Llanfair, the rails through the streets at Portmadoc, and the site of the Welsh Highland Railway stations – so I travelled first on the Festiniog on an evening train headed by *Prince*, which had to stop for a 'blow-up' near the cemetery. Next day I travelled in the wet on the Talyllyn in a packed train and stayed in a bed and breakfast near Pendre, before obtaining permission to camp near Brynglas for a couple of nights. I then decided to join the TRPS rather than the FRS and volunteered for traffic duties, progressing to Guard within a week. Summer visits continued and I camped at Brynglas in my little ex-US Army tent. At this time we also often went in after the trains had finished running to carry out minor repairs on the carriages. I also became acquainted with Edward Thomas, who was secretary of Bethany English Presbyterian Church; he discovered that I was a theology student and I was summoned to see him in the old Haydn Jones office above the Post Office, where he attended to the business of the estate. He persuaded me to take a service at Bethany from time to time, which I have done ever since. He would always ask, 'How's the little railway?' which embarrassed me as I knew he was a Director, lived next door to Wharf station at 'Trefri' and walked across the bridge to his office each day. His niece, Zella, besides being the Abergynolwyn tea lady, was Treasurer at Bethany and sometimes played the organ, although she was too short to reach the pedals.

My first articles and letters appeared in *Talyllyn News*, and after I started work I graduated to staying in a bed and breakfast, either with Mrs Jones at 'Monfa', or Mrs Clifford in Idris Villas. She had been a driver of racing cars in the 1930s and did not understand trains, but went to a dentist in Barmouth and was terrified by the journey across the Friog cliff, where the train went very slowly with alarming noises on the somewhat uncertain track; her fears were not allayed by the tales told by her Talyllyn visitors of the trains that had fallen off on to the beach.

I started going to winter working parties for carriage repairs and painting, under the able guidance of Keith Walton, and also became the East Midlands representative on the Midlands Area Committee; this eventually became a separate group, which persuaded me to stand for Council, and I served from 1974 to 1984. In 1965 I was a founder member of the Traffic & Operating Committee and helped organise the first training courses for traffic staff at various venues in England. Membership of this group also led me to take a leading role in the redesign of the tickets, which became necessary as the traditional ticket printers closed down due to falling demand for Edmondson card tickets. The new series was introduced in 1967 and included provision for Nant Gwernol issues. In recent years I have been printing tickets myself and organising supplies, so the stock is gradually reverting to something closer to the unified pattern adopted in 1967.

On getting married I used a bequest from my grandparents to purchase a property in Tywyn, so the town became even more of a home from home as I moved from place to place with my work. While in Milton Keynes I found that one of the secondary schools there had a 'Week Ten', when students who were up to date with their academic work could choose what activity they wished to follow. Several groups travelled with me to the TR over the years and undertook tasks such as extending the platforms at Rhydyronen and installing the skylight and booking office at Dolgoch. At this time I learned to drive diesel locos and did so for many years on works trains. One of the things I have always done is to introduce people of all ages, but especially young people, to the TR, and I still do this; it has usually been a very rewarding experience all round.

When I retired from Council, Graham Vincent invited me to become active in the Narrow Gauge Railway Museum, and this involvement continues to the present time, although no longer in an official capacity since the redevelopment work, but in maintaining and restoring the Trust's two operational diesel locos at North Ings Farm and in populating and maintaining the website. On retiring as a trustee I found that for the first time in 40 years I was no longer a member of any committee connected with the TR. I can look back on so many projects, including two illustrated booklets, *The Nant Gwernol Extension* in 1977 and *Forty Years of the Talyllyn Railway* in 1991: 50 years as a Talyllyn Guard, with a great retirement day on 31 December 2010; so many people, from Edward and Zella Thomas to paid staff and fellow volunteers of all ages and all walks of life, some just discovering the Talyllyn for the first time; too many wonderful experiences to even recall; and gratitude that I joined the Society – even now there are not many days when I don't do something for the Talyllyn.

David Leech

The first time I saw the Talyllyn Railway was in 1955 on a trip from the school Railway Society. The coach company must have been one of the first to make the classic mistake of quoting for the journey to the wrong Towyn, the one on the North Wales coast. At that time they were both spelled 'Towyn', but the Merioneth one was 'Towyn-on-Sea'. Three Bedford OBs set out in convoy from Manchester with the coach company agreeing to maintain the quoted price and the drivers determined to achieve the original timings.

In Corwen one of the vehicles lost a water plug and there was a delay whilst the local blacksmith replaced it. As we passed through Bala, a police sergeant in a light blue Morris Minor stopped us for speeding and there was another delay while he sharpened his pencil.

Wharf station at Towyn in about 1956, showing the original brick building. The train on the left is made up of loco No 3 *Sir Haydn* (built in 1876), one original TR coach and the first two bogie coaches from 1954. The train on the right is made up of loco No 6 *Douglas* (built in 1918), which was a gift to the TR from Abelsons (a Birmingham plant firm), three original TR coaches, an open from Penrhyn Quarry, and the original TR guard's van (Van 5), built in 1865. *John Adams, TR Collection*

Volunteers' stories

Our arrival at Wharf station was met with much shouting from railway staff as we ran headlong down the drive and were bundled into an original TR carriage, the train making its first lurch forward before the door was shut.

And that is all I remember. As soon as we arrived back at Wharf we were chased onto the coaches, as the vehicles were required in Manchester for an evening job. There was no time to look at anything – the TR motive power could have been a green horse for all I knew. The railway must have left some impression, however, because we went on a family holiday to Towyn in 1957. Staying at 'Monfa' on Pier Road, Mrs Jones was my first introduction to an iconic Tywyn TR landlady who was to become such a good friend to so many volunteers over the years.

Seriously starting railway volunteering in 1958, I received my 'Learner Guard' card in July 1959 and my 'Qualified Guard' card at the end of the fortnight's stay. The verbal citation from Harold Parker as he gave me my card was, 'You may as well have this as you've been doing the job for a year, and besides there's nobody else at the moment.' Clearly, retrospective issue of grade cards, even then, was a TR tradition. There was some training. Generally, you were learning from someone who had started just before you had; all the training was on the job and more often than not was a voyage of discovery for both Guard and Learner.

Wharf office was the original brick building with the access door at the Pendre end. It was divided into two by a central wall containing a door and a fireplace with, usually, a blazing coal fire whatever the weather. Through the door in the other half was the weighing machine; outside the window the weighing platform was still rail-connected, and the siding still in use. Wharf drive was narrow between grass verges, and the public wandered down and into the office. They stood at a high counter to buy their tickets, half-a-crown return to Abergynolwyn. If they wanted to visit the shop they shuffled left two paces, the shop being a cardboard box with Kit-Kats and later a postcard. In early days, on reporting for duty – or 'turning up', as it was termed then – for the duration of the shift you were issued with a uniform jacket made of thin light grey material. On wet days, if you were on two trips you put the wet jacket over a chair in front of the fire and took another from the hook behind the door.

Your kit consisted of some tickets, a pair of clippers, a plain 'Cathedral' carbon copy book and some change. Included in the change were two pennies. If you ran into trouble up the line and all else failed, you made your way to the valley road and hitched a lift to the nearest phone box. The train log was made up in the carbon copy book with the usual information – date, train time, loco, driver, fireman, guard, and so on. Then the stations to Abergynolwyn and back were listed down the left-hand side and passing or stopping times entered as they occurred. At the end of the day, cash taken was noted with the Guard's signature. In the office, the top copy was taken out and filed and the book with the second copy put ready for the next day. For a period Guards were instructed to write 'right time throughout' instead of listing stations and times, if they could do so with a reasonably clear conscience. I think everybody was glad when we were instructed to revert to the original system. It was much more fun being able to compare other people's days on the copy, and previous logs were often a good guide as to what to do when faced with an unusual situation.

Having checked in at Wharf, you walked up the track to Pendre, where were located the original carriage shelter and loco shed with a cottage forming the back half of the shed at the roadside. The road over the level crossing was narrow with gates to suit. Herbert and Margaret Jones lived in the cottage, and Margaret would attend to the gates when she heard the train whistling. When Margaret was away word would go round that you worked your own gates. With a handbrake on the loco and in the guard's van and nothing in between, it was unwise to assume, whatever the situation, that the gates would be open by the time you reached them.

Train preparation started with looking for couplings, in case your train became divided. The carriages were coupled with a hook and shackle and a link. The shackle was thrown over one carriage hook and a link placed over the other, the downward-facing hook on the shackle then being dropped into the link. It was necessary to match the coupling combination with the space between the coaches such that the buffers were held tight together on the straight – not always easy when spaces and link lengths were all different. You had to watch out for one particularly long link, which, if the train braked and the coaches closed up, would ride up the coach hook and slip off – I once looked back on a down train slowing for Dolgoch and saw 15 feet of daylight between the two halves of the train. In the down direction the brake-van was next to the loco and it was possible to alert the crew, so a very gradual stop reunited the two halves of the train with an acceptable bump and nobody was any the wiser.

Once the train was coupled it was swept out with a bald brush, and Brasso applied to the door handles. This was followed by Oiling Up. The axle boxes on the coaches had a hinged lid, under which was a compartment that held the oil.

oilcan. Later, the Corris coach had small holes in each axle box with, at first, a cork stopper, so the traffic oilcan came into its own and broke. Then you had to borrow the loco oilcan and give a solemn undertaking that you would refill it, as 12 axle boxes emptied it completely.

At this time your driver would usually be Hugh or Herbert Jones, Bill Faulkner, Gareth Jones ('Monfa') and later Dai Jones. Any of them would willingly help a struggling Guard and

Loco No 4 *Edward Thomas* arrives at Abergynolwyn in the early days of the Society running the railway. *TR Collection*

From this reservoir a small hole fed the oil to the journal almost as fast as you put it in. The oil was fed into the axle box from a large white enamel jug by way of a 'shoe' (a metal chute enlarged at one end); it was poured into the larger end, the other end being directed into the axle box. One TR coach was different, in that each axle box had a bulge on the side with a hole in the top and oil was dribbled into each hole from an ordinary

chances were that the Guard would be helping them before the day was out. Gareth Jones was a Fireman on British Railways' Cambrian line, and at times when the TR was short of drivers he would be relieved at Towyn Wharf (BR) by another BR fireman so that he could drive the afternoon TR train from Towyn Wharf (TR).

Trains were propelled from Pendre to Wharf. There were no token machines and only one telephone, so the arrival of the empty stock always came as a relief to the staff on duty at Wharf. On very rare occasions the empty coaches arrived before the loco. The Guard always stopped the coaches in time with his handbrake, but it was

Volunteers' stories

considered best practice for everything to arrive together and the locomotives were the first to be equipped with dedicated screw couplings. Occasionally, departure from Wharf would be preceded by the loco crew sanding the rails for a good distance and starting as far back down the platform as possible to get a run at the bank. If this procedure failed, you simply backed down and tried again.

The last task before leaving Wharf was to check that you had Miss Thomas on board. Miss Thomas was the 'Refreshment Lady' of Reverend Awdry fame. Small, mild but determined, she ran up the platform at the last minute, her hair done up tightly in a bun, pink overall flying and cash box tucked firmly under her arm. It was easy to leave her behind, and if you did you had to stop halfway out of the station to pick her up. Every Guard I knew left her behind at some time, driving Harold Parker to apoplexy.

Out on the line speeds were lower than today but the ride was far livelier. Hogged rails, pumping sleepers, lack of ballast and grabbing brambles made the experience interesting until you got used to it. However, I have never experienced a derailment to a passenger train in service and I only know one Guard who has. There were no manned stations up the line; in fact, there were no offices to man, and the Guard covered all ticket sales including the terminus at Abergynolwyn. As virtually all traffic originated at Towyn, the biggest problem for the Guard was achieving an arrival time back at Wharf that would ensure that connections were made to the British Railways trains at Towyn in both directions, as a large proportion of the passengers arrived by rail. It was possible to have the BR trains held for a few minutes if necessary as Towyn station was fully staffed, complete with signal box, and the concept of service to the passenger was absolute. Conversely, Talyllyn trains were held if BR trains were delayed, the BR request being relayed to Wharf including how many passengers there were for interchange.

In the early days the timetable consisted of one morning round trip and two trains in the afternoon: the express, which carried boards stating 'Dolgoch and Abergynolwyn only', left Wharf at 2.10pm, and the 'all stations', left at three o'clock. The length of time between departures allowed for shunting the first train out of the way at Abergynolwyn; the short platform ending at the top of the drive was barely long enough to hold one train. After the run-round loop, the line continued up the Extension, over a stone slab culvert past the gatepost and open gate marking the limit of passenger-carrying, and through the Winding House at the head of the village incline to the foot of the first quarry incline. Odd lengths of rail were missing above the Winding House, but marks in the grass suggested that rail wheels passed below there occasionally.

On arrival at Abergynolwyn the loco on the first afternoon train ran round and propelled the train up the Extension far enough to give the following train room to run round. Meanwhile, in the station building, which consisted of the standard shelter and room, the latter had been unlocked to reveal a gas fridge and a gas ring for a large kettle. Miss Thomas's first task was to light the fridge; it was only lit when trains were present, for economy reasons. This involved kneeling in front of it and poking a lighted match in the right place. Usually there was a soft pop and all was well. Occasionally the earth shook and Miss Thomas appeared very annoyed and somewhat flushed. The ice-cream, which had accompanied her from Wharf, was put in the freezer to be sold as soon as it had solidified again. Cups of tea were dispensed from a huge enamel teapot, and so was born the tradition of serving refreshments at Abergynolwyn. There were of course no toilets – when trains were busy and passengers spread all over the area, the train crews would climb on the loco and discreetly drift down the line until out of sight round the first bend, returning very relieved a few minutes later – and all done without even a 'Shunt into section'.

The return workings of the two afternoon trains were operated on the time interval system. The express, 'Dolgoch and Wharf only', left at 4.45pm and the following all-stations had to wait 15 minutes before leaving Abergynolwyn. After a hurried ticket check at Dolgoch, the express guard would write the departure time of his train on a piece of paper and leave it under a stone on the seat in the station shelter. The guard of the following train waited until 15 minutes after the time on the paper before flagging his train away. The snags with this system are obvious, and the express guard always kept a good lookout to the rear, even when running normally.

There was also a greater hazard. With trains being so full, there were invariably passengers left at Dolgoch for the following train, the express guard not having time to argue, and they were always interested in the piece of paper. Consequently, it often blew away, got lost, or on one occasion was eaten by a dog. Technology came to the rescue and a small wooden box with a locking lid and a slot for the paper was screwed to the shelter wall. Years after, when time interval was a memory, the box was still emptied as it was frequently mistaken for a donation box.

There were occasions when two passenger trains were crossed at Brynglas. If you were available as a spare guard, you would travel on the first train with a padlock key and small red and green flags, and base yourself in the station shelter for the day. The first job was to securely wedge your packed lunch in the roof truss in the shelter to prevent the farm dog eating it while your back was turned. Second, the loop had to be cleared of any pigs asleep between the rails on the sun-warmed ballast. The dog was no help, but a tap with a flagstick usually worked. Brynglas loop was on the down side of the platform and shelter, separated from it by a farm track crossing the rails. As on the rest of the railway, the points were operated by throw-over dollies mounted on the point sleepers. For facing operation, the point lock consisted of a swivel hasp and staple so arranged that the tongue of the hasp would hold the point blade against the stock rail, the hasp being passed over the staple and locked with a padlock. The third job was to check that you had been given the right key for the padlocks, one at each end of the loop. Then, with the dog and maybe a pig for company, you settled down to wait.

Towards the time you had been told the crossing was to take place, you started listening for train sounds and trying to work out which would be the first arrival. There were no stop boards and trains would stop fairly close to the points. When the first train came into sight, you went to each loop point, unlocked it, threw it over and locked it again. Then the train was allowed into the loop. As soon as it had stopped, you again went to each point, unlocked it, threw it over, relocked it, and signalled the other train to pass. The drivers exchanged tokens and any other information, cab to cab, as the locomotives passed. After the trains had departed you set and locked

Tea break at Abergynolwyn is now a far cry from the early days when there were no toilets and refreshments were ice-creams re-frozen in a gas freezer! Every down train has a stop at Abergynolwyn for toilets and refreshments, and here *Sir Haydn* **simmers while the crew join the passengers in having a break.** *TR Collection*

the road for the main line. You then retired to the shelter to wait for the train back to Wharf and threw bits of ballast at the pig.

Of course, it wasn't all work. On the evenings when we weren't working to repair some piece of equipment vital for next day's operation, there was a variety of activities on offer. One evening two of us emptied a BR wagon of spent ballast while a growing crowd gathered on Wharf road bridge to watch. As dusk fell, a member of the crowd appeared on the Wharf edge with a paper bag of money he had collected from the crowd. We waved our thanks; they gave us a round of applause and went their separate ways. On other nights, we would wander down the promenade and watch the country dancing through the front-room window of the Christian Endeavour Holiday Home. On Sundays, as Towyn was dry, we had to get the last train out to Barmouth to get a drink, making sure we didn't miss the last one back.

It couldn't go on. There were two preserved railways, the Festiniog and the TR, and at that time the TR was receiving all the 'operated by volunteers' glory and publicity. Traffic was growing incredibly and the old problem was always present: revenue from passengers was barely sufficient to cover wear and tear and some essential additional equipment. One day, on the last train down, I had 27 passengers in the TR brake-van. On other occasions, after the last arrival of the day at Wharf, the whole train would be propelled back to Dolgoch to pick up the 40 or so passengers who had had to wait. It was obvious that the railway had to change to offer the growing number of passengers a safe and acceptable ride.

I think that we all knew that the early days could not last. We had the experience of operating a traditional minor railway that was changing before our eyes as it became more popular. It grew and developed into what was necessary to survive in a commercial world with modern legislation and practices. The early days can never be recreated because the conditions will never exist again. It was an unrepeatable, unique experience.

John Gott

The early days of volunteering were for me a pretty amazing time of growing up and finding a place in the world, transforming me from a shy and introverted only child into a young man with friends, a degree of independence, a shared purpose and a sense of achievement (albeit still on the shy side!). But shyness is relative: becoming a TR Guard at 15, responsible for the safety and well-being of a trainload of 200-plus strangers and for dealing with, in those days, the fairly frequent occasions when operating a railway didn't always go quite to plan certainly gave me the self-confidence to move straight from school to shift working in the Parcels Office at Northampton Castle station, not a location for shrinking violets!

I had one holiday as an Assistant Guard before getting my own trains the following Easter, by far the most terrifying being a ballast train empty from Pendre to Quarry Siding, loaded on site, then back to Pendre. At that time relationships between the various branches of the railway were not as inclusive as today; loco crew and guards coexisted happily enough, but the brawny, hearty track gangs tended to look down on us weedy traffic staff. To emphasise this hierarchy, I was 'encouraged' to help load the wagons at Quarry Siding but, having allowed an impossibly big metal wheelbarrow full of wet shale to run away with me and veer sideways off the plank walkway, I was dispatched in disgrace back to the guard's van to allow the real men to get on with the job.

Health & Safety was then but a gleam in some youthful bureaucrat's eye. No 10 (the semi-open 'Stanton Van') had a small guard's compartment from which one emerged after passing under Wharf bridge to edge down the footboard clipping tickets while keeping one arm looped round the roof supports. It was of course critical to complete the task before arriving at Ffordd Cadfan bridge. The time thus saved was used to ensure that the train was as full as possible on departure; the booking clerk's clicker

Loco No 5 *Midlander* approaches Quarry Siding Halt with Van 5 in the early days of the Society. *TR Collection*

was used not for statistical interest but to avoid over-booking a train before its arrival. We would run into Wharf (controlled purely by the loco handbrake) and see an anxious queue of potential passengers winding up the slope in the hope of being able to travel. After booked passengers had found seats, the Guard would count up those left vacant (three a side in the TRs and, for a 1st Class supplement, the Glyn Valleys, four a side elsewhere), give the magic number to the booking clerk, then fit the passengers in, splitting up groups as necessary. It wasn't uncommon to run through Rhydyronen non-stop – the hand signal for 'full up', incidentally, is the lower arm waved horizontally, palm downwards.

There was of course less control over the loading of the last down train, and station time at Dolgoch (then a much more popular destination than today) to sort everyone out was constrained by the BR connection and the need to ensure that through passengers had priority. A volunteer's car sometimes had to be dispatched to Dolgoch to bring back to civilisation those unable to squeeze on, while on a few particularly crowded days the other train set, propelled empty from Brynglas, worked an extra train back. It was not unknown for a suitably nubile young lady to be invited onto the engine to (marginally) ease the shortage of seats, while my own record from Dolgoch was 28 passengers in the TR Van, which rather precluded balancing the ticket money before arrival at Wharf.

Expectations were lower in those days, time not so precious, and the TR virtually unique, so any grumbling was rare.

Couplings were all hook and link, the art being, with a finite supply of each, to keep every coupling on both train sets as tight as possible. On one occasion my down train restarted from Rhydyronen with enough of a snatch to cause a hook in the middle of the set to drop off its link. Alerted by the train alarm parting, Dai Jones slowed down enough to allow the errant rear coaches to buffer up relatively gently, I recoupled almost before the train had stopped, and we were on our way again. As it happened, a visiting group of Festiniog management were seated just by the break and later professed themselves surprised

Volunteers' stories

and impressed by the lack of any lengthy inquest attending the incident.

Trains were crossed at Brynglas, using a train staff and tickets to avoid any chance of a single-line collision and a padlocked hasp on the relevant sleeper to lock the facing point at each end of the loop. No accommodation was provided for the guard spending the day at Brynglas, and certainly nothing as cissy as a toilet. A deckchair was available for sunny days, the main hazard being that one would be slumbering peacefully when the trains optimistically hoping to cross turned up. Choosing their victim with some care (the guard who always carried an alarm clock was an unlikely prospect), Herbert or Dai on a down train used to coast down to the stop-board in complete silence, then open the steam cocks, hang on the whistle and beat the shovel on the footplate.

Health & Safety might also have looked askance a few years later when the construction of a block post at Quarry Siding allowed my girlfriend (now wife – intermarriage was another occasional consequence of the influx of volunteers into the area) and me to get a camping stove going on the floor so that, as well as the token, I could hand over freshly fried jam doughnuts to passing train crews. Those in charge at Wharf turned a blind eye (and open mouth) to this enterprise.

Do I have any claims to fame? Modestly, I must admit that I do: as well as the masterful whistle on 'The Old Lady Drives to Dolgoch', I appear in one of the Reverend Awdry's stories – but I'll leave you to work out which!

John Smallwood

Saturday 22 August 1959 found the Smallwood family setting out from Beckenham in south-east London in father's 1935 Rolls-Royce (it was the only vehicle large enough to carry Mum, Dad and us five kids!) for our annual summer holiday – this year in Aberdovey. I seem to remember we broke our journey in Kidderminster for some reason. So we arrived in Aberdovey on Sunday to find our holiday guest house in Gwelfor Terrace overlooking the tennis courts and railway station – a grandstand view of the steam trains on the Cambrian Coast line. The guest house was run by Mr and Mrs Lewis. Geoff Lewis was, by a lucky chance, one of the signalmen at Tywyn BR station, so I was made welcome in the signal box before finding my way down

John Smallwood, then and now! *John Smallwood collection*

to the TR's Wharf station. As I walked down the slope the first train I saw on the TR appeared under the bridge headed by No 4, bunker first of course. And a big surprise – the fireman was a lady! Ann Carter, as I later found out, was the daughter of one of the engineering volunteers and no stranger to steam. In those days No 4 still had its original cramped Corris cab and Ann clearly had difficulty in moving comfortably around in the confines of the little engine. I forget who the driver was, but I expect it was either Dai Jones or Bill Faulkner. The guard, to whom I was soon introduced by the genial and very Welsh General Manager Harold Parker, was one Barry Lomas.

Harold Parker, presiding over the cramped office accommodation in the original building – which is now about half of the shop – made me very welcome and allowed me to travel with Barry to start learning the complexities of guarding a Talyllyn train. The van was the original Talyllyn van – No 5 – which I was to get to know intimately over the coming years! It was customary to guard the train, if the weather was kind, from a position sitting on the floor of the van between the sliding doors, with your feet on the footboard – probably not official, but accepted by all. In fact, I must admit that given half a chance I still do that to this day when guarding from Van 5! Indeed, I well recall that some years later, when David Woodhouse had taken over from Harold as General Manager, I had been guarding from the same van and had returned my ticket box and waybill to the office. As I turned to leave the office the stern Birmingham tones of David rang out: 'You've been sitting on the van step,' he accused. There was a big dirty patch on the back of my trousers! I was pleased to note in that classic TR film *Railway with a Heart of Gold*, made in 1953, that there is a shot of David Woodhouse guarding, and also sitting on the van step. But I am rushing ahead with my memories.

In my first week I also learned about guarding from Keith Stretch. On the locomotives I met Dai and Herbert Jones and Bill Faulkner driving.

No 6 *Douglas*, driven by Charlie Daniel, is seen at Brynglas, heading a 'double header' with Keith Foster visible on the second loco, and Guard Andy Young standing on the footboard of the original TR guard's van No 5. *TR collection*

Volunteers' stories

Those who keep TR rolling stock in good repair are known as the 'bodgers'. Here in the early 1970s John Smallwood, a volunteer for more than 50 years, re-seals the roof of one of the original TR coaches. *TR Collection*

I particularly remember firemen Bert Brock, Ann Carter, Phil Glazebrook and Harold Vickers, who succeeded in derailing No 6 one day in 1960 twice on the same points outside the south carriage shed. Dai and I became great friends and I well recall a few years later finding him in the engine shed one Monday after I had arrived on the Saturday. 'I knew you were here, John,' beamed Dai. 'The ends of the carriages have been cleaned!' So things haven't changed much to this day. I hope I have succeeded in encouraging today's young and not so young guards to pay attention to the ends of the coaches.

On my second working visit, in August 1960, when I walked in to the office I was met with a smile from Harold Parker. 'Oh, I'm glad you are here, John,' he said. 'We need a guard tomorrow!' Promotion was rather less formal in those days! Sure enough, next day, Thursday 25 August 1960, I was rostered to guard on my own the 1.15pm train, which according to the Train Book was the Bogie Train – Cardboard Carriages 9 and 10 in their pre-standard body state and probably TR 4 and the Corris Van for luggage, etc. The Train Book doesn't detail what was added to the two bogies, but I have a photograph of the 10.25am train on the same day, which was a right mixed formation – from the front, the Corris van, followed by a TR, Glyn, two opens, two more TRs and the two bogies. So no doubt the two afternoon trains were made up of bits of this ensemble! My engine was No 4, driven by Bill Faulkner with Hugh Eaves (who moved up to Portmadoc in later years) firing. This was the first time my name appeared in the Train Book, of which I have a photocopy courtesy of Dolgellau Archives. I was then rostered to guard on all my subsequent visits.

In 1963 I asked Harold Parker if I could have a Guard's card. He looked astonished. 'Haven't you got one?' he asked. So my original card (No 22) is dated 7 September 1963. In 1968 cards were reissued and, being in the right place at the right time, I was issued with No 1 of the new series! I'm proud of both of them. My visits from 1959 were only for my annual Traffic Duties and most AGMs, but in 1966 Phil Glazebrook persuaded me to visit in the winter and I started joining the London Area working parties from time to time. I well remember my first one, leaving Edgware in a long-wheelbase Land Rover at about 5.00pm and eventually arriving in Tywyn at about 1.30am. On that particular cold night we found the road from Dinas Mawddwy to Cross Foxes to be surrounded by deep snow and in the full moon it was a beautiful sight.

From 1961 I stayed at 11 Cambrian Terrace with Mr and Mrs Ivor Jones ('the Gas'). I became one of the family there until I moved to Tywyn in 1988 having taken early retirement from the Big Railway. One memorable day was probably in the late 1970s. Richard Martindale and I were the regular carriage bodging gang in those days and we visited at least once a month to work on the carriages. I carried on through the 1980s and 1990s as Chief Bodger, leading the carriage refurbishing gang. Mrs Jones had a B&B sign in her window, but rarely had any casual visitors, so one morning Richard and I were surprised to find strangers at the breakfast table. Mrs Jones asked them if they would like some toast. Richard and I looked at each other in disbelief. We had never been offered toast. Foolishly we commented on that fact. Mona Jones looked sternly at us. 'You don't want toast!' she ordered. But toast arrived and heaven help us during future visits if we didn't eat it all! And Ivor used to sit there watching HTV all the time: 'Ivor – turn the sound down!' and 'Ivor, turn the television off – John doesn't want to watch that rubbish!' when the only interesting programme started.

Oh yes, being a TR volunteer has had its moments – and not just meeting Prince Charles on two occasions. I was honoured to be elected to the Council of the Talyllyn Railway Preservation Society in 1974, and was re-elected every other year until 2010, when I decided to retire. In addition, for the last few of those 36 years I was also on the Board of Talyllyn Holdings. Between 2001 and 2004 I was Project Manager for the new Wharf Station, during which time I had great support in particular from David Mitchell. Peter Austin took over from me then to supervise the actual construction phase, for which I was truly grateful! There have been moments, but most of the time it's been great fun – all 52 years of it! I only hope that despite the heavy government involvement these days today's youngsters have as much fun as I have had. I wouldn't have missed it all for anything.

Gordon Rhodes

I joined the TRPS following family holidays in Wales in 1955 and 1957, but it was not until 1960 that I could afford the £25 that two weeks volunteering would cost me. I travelled on the 'Cambrian Coast Express' from Paddington to stay with Gwen and Hughie Jones at 'Monfa' on Pier Road, as their advertisement stated that they had electricity and inside sanitation, which made me wonder what the rest of Towyn was like. On that first Sunday morning I drew back the curtains of my second-floor bedroom window to behold a herd of cattle wandering down the road towards the beach and decided there and then that if this was typical of Towyn then it was going to be great.

After breakfast I went to Wharf and introduced myself to Harold Parker, the General Manager, who instructed me to go to Pendre and find Douglas Maas, as I was to be his assistant guard. Shunting, coupling, cleaning and oiling were all a blur, as was our one trip up the line, but the shock came on our return to Wharf, when Harold informed me that Douglas was going home that evening and I was the guard for the rest of the week.

1960 was the last year when cleaning and oiling of stock was carried out in the very confined space of the unlit original south carriage shed prior to its rebuilding, where carriage doors would only half open and oil was administered

Volunteers' stories

to axle boxes using a large jug and a metal chute. Couplings were hooks and links, which were varied to suit differing lengths of buffers and shapes of carriage hooks; this wasn't too bad until an extra vehicle was added, when swapping of the ironmongery took place. These additional vehicles meant a run up to Pendre, as none were kept at Wharf even though a siding was available, so life could be hectic if we had a sudden rush of passengers. Advice and instruction from Dai and Herbert Jones, sometimes in explicit terms, together with a similar sense of humour, really helped me through that first week without making too many mistakes, and the arrival of John Brown made the second week more relaxed as I was now in the company of an old hand with a year of volunteering behind him. John was a master at people-packing – it seemed he could make passengers actually want to sit 'four a side, children on laps with bags, pushchairs and dogs under seats', and his passenger chat while checking tickets proved a very hard act to follow. He later joined the permanent staff for a while, but unfortunately died at an early age and a great character was lost.

My learning curve was nearly vertical, having to cope with just a £1 cash float in the van, dodgy door handles and passengers who all seemed to want to return on the last train. If there were passengers at any of the stations up the line, which were all unmanned, change for their fares could exhaust the float and it was then a matter of persuasion or pleading to get the correct money, and the cash overs and unders record book at Wharf seemed to be in daily use. The four TR carriages were not fitted with positive lock door handles and a keen watch had to be kept on them, hoping that they would not vibrate open before the next station stop – if they did, the only way of stopping the train was to wind on the handbrake, wave a red flag and blow a whistle, though if the fireman was remonstrating with his recalcitrant steed it could be some time before he looked back.

Some days it became very apparent that more passengers were being taken up the line than were returning, which was a sign that the last down train was going to be interesting as we could usually clear Abergynolwyn platform but not have room for those at Dolgoch. With luck the telephone system would be working and Wharf informed of the situation. However, with some cable strung in the hedgerows or lying on the ground, where a species of Welsh rodent had taken a dietary liking to cable insulation, on occasion a quick trip to the telephone in Aber village was called for; I only did this once and had a lift from a passenger who had his car nearby. At Dolgoch fun would be had trying to get passengers to relinquish their seats in favour of those with tickets for main-line trains with which we made a connection, and even with the promise of an extra train we would leave the station with quite a number of standing passengers. All this would take time and ticket checking was abandoned, with the result that we would stop at all the intermediate stations to set down any passengers; upon arrival at Brynglas the crew of the relief train would be informed that only Dolgoch required clearing, so they would run their loco to the rear of their train and propel it up the line, as this was before Quarry Siding had a loop. All good fun…

Gordon Rhodes. *Nigel Adams*

Gordon Rhodes: the 1860 date is deliberate!
Nigel Adams

It has been known to rain in Tywyn on occasion, and when the empty stock for the first up train arrived at Wharf the assembled passengers quickly took their seats. One of the vehicles was No 18, and as it had been left outside overnight the glass bowls attached to the inside of the roof to simulate removed oil light fittings had partly filled with water from small leaks in the said roof. The bedraggled guard was aware of this situation and, waiting until the windows were well steamed up, he opened the door and with an 'Excuse me' to the startled and soggy passengers, drained the bowl's contents into a bucket and closed the door with a 'Thank you'. When the stock arrived at Wharf the next morning it had mysteriously gained a goldfish carved from a carrot, which lazily swam around the bowl for the rest of the day.

Part way through my 1963 session on the railway Harold Parker informed me that I must have a guard's grade card, and I was instructed to write to David Woodhouse, who held the Traffic Section records, and state that Harold Parker said that I should be issued with one. No formal training, no assessments, one trip as an assistant – just use your initiative and get on with the job.

Perhaps my most hectic day on the railway was August Bank Holiday Monday 1966, with David Hume from Aberdovey as my assistant. There were no morning trains, and those in the afternoon were at 1.10, 2.10, 3.10 and 4.10. John Brown was Guard of the first set with No 4 driven by Bill Faulkner; being full, it was banked up the cutting by No 1 driven by Dai Jones, with Roy Smith firing, who then backed their loco onto our set at Pendre. As we had been warned that a lot of passengers were already at Wharf, we had No 6 leading us down the cutting so it could bank us back to Pendre. Volunteers were holding back the crowd on the platform and as soon as we stopped all the seats were filled including the TR van, with two passengers in the van booking office; they only moved out when I threatened not to start the train until we had unrestricted access to the handbrake, which David then manned with me riding on the footboard. We had a 10-minute wait at Brynglas for the down train, decanted a lot of passengers at Dolgoch and, with a now empty van, arrived at Abergynolwyn about 5 minutes late. For our return trip we managed to find every passenger a seat and departed for Dolgoch on time, where the platform was heaving and it was people-packing to the limit. We abandoned ticket checking in favour of stopping at the intermediate stations, which was going to increase our already late running; we were at Brynglas before the 3.10 up train, which steamed through late behind No 4 with a grinning Bill Faulkner and consisting of its normal set, all the spare stock and John Brown in a happy mood. Arrival at Wharf was behind time and, with the platform still crowded even that late in the afternoon, it was a case of finding seats (including the van), checking tickets and, after some loco shuffling, setting off again with No 2 driven by Geoff Hayes at the front, and No 6, with Herbert driving, as banker as far as Quarry Siding. Hugh Eaves was the fireman on No 2 with Alan Barrett on No 6, so you can tell it wasn't yesterday.

The run up was much the same as our first, but clearing Abergynolwyn was interesting and we left with four-a-side, standing passengers and 15 in the van, with the prospect of Dolgoch looming before us. Our train made a connection with the Cambrian at the BR station, so it was a case of persuading some passengers to wait for the inevitable relief train in favour of those with

Volunteers' stories

main-line tickets; this all took time but, with the knowledge that there were no intermediate passengers, we set off rather late with David still in the booking office, myself standing with both feet on the footboard and 20 passengers in the van. By the time we arrived at Brynglas No 6 was ready to propel the relief train up the line so, after telling the loco crew that only Dolgoch needed clearing, we set off at a smart pace for Wharf. When you consider that neither Dolgoch nor Abergynolwyn was manned in those halcyon days, it was gratifying to be told that our cash takings actually balanced at the end of the day. By the time Alan Barrett had disposed of No 6 at Pendre it was quite late in the evening, and we climbed into his car for the journey, devoid of motorways and with only a short section of dual carriageway, back to south London, arriving at 2.45am. What a great day, but my liking of van No 5 had diminished somewhat.

The west-end points at Abergynolwyn were at one time controlled by a single lever locked with an Annetts key carried in the guard's van, which, when inserted into the base of the ground frame and turned, unlocked the lever. This was all very relevant as, when leaving Wharf for my first trip up the line one year, someone shouted, 'Look out for the hornets!', which I took as a reference to the latest unfathomable 'in' joke, but on arrival at Abergynolwyn all was revealed. A swarm of hornets had decided that the lever ground frame was a good place to set up home and definitely did not want to be disturbed. Unfortunately the dreaded combination of Dai Jones and Hugh Eaves were on No 1 and took great delight in explaining that an expert was on his way to deal with the situation but would not be arriving until the next day and they were very quick in bringing the loco to the west end of the loop as they wanted to see the fun. For the uninitiated a hornet is like a very large wasp but with kamikaze tendencies and best given a very wide berth. So, with much encouragement from the footplate, I ran towards the frame, pushed in the key, continued in a westerly direction, turned at a safe distance and waited for the hornets to calm down. Eastbound, I managed to turn the key and paused before again running past and pushing the lever, thus setting the road for the loop. As the loco ran past me, I noticed that the bemused passengers who had been watching the performance had, on being informed of the situation by the loco crew, retreated to the far end of the platform. My bi-directional running resumed until the loco was coupled to the brake van with the point relocked, key safely in the van and the loco crew, happily for

Loco No 6 *Douglas* **heads a train at Abergynolwyn around 1960, and is about to run round its train, as this was the terminus of the line until 1976. The west-end ground frame is out of sight beyond the train. The driver, seen to the left of the loco, is the late Lord Northesk, who was one of the early volunteers.** *John Adams, TR Collection*

me, now nearest the ground frame. It is the only time that I have received a round of applause from passengers; as for the hornets, they were to be removed early the next morning, but somehow we forgot to tell the first-turn guard.

As any traffic volunteer on the railway will tell you, our passengers can at times unwittingly provide us with endless amusement, amazement or frustration, which adds greatly to the fun of running the railway. We had just left Wharf one day and were heading up the cutting when passengers' heads and waving arms appeared from several windows of a bogie vehicle, and they obviously wanted the train to stop. Due to the location this was not going to happen, but when we arrived at Pendre platform doors flew open and several people dashed past me heading down the track towards Wharf before they could be stopped. One of them paused briefly to say that they had left the baby in a carry-cot in the shop and it later transpired that as they were spread out in different compartments each thought the other had the infant. Sure enough it was found sleeping soundly and I often wondered what the Wharf office incumbents would have made of that piece of lost property.

It wasn't really my fault that Miss Thomas was left behind at Wharf, as I had seen her board the train but not alight to go into the shop. Diminutive Miss Zella Thomas, a niece of Edward Thomas, was a determined chapel member, in charge of the Tea Van that was taken up to Aber on the first train of the day. She was normally very quietly spoken, perhaps demure, though not averse to a quick cigarette behind the Tea Van when she thought nobody was looking. We had to wait for her at Pendre while she staggered up the cutting breathing more fire and brimstone than a Welsh dragon and with language that would have put a Liverpool docker to shame, so after that I always made certain that she was on the train.

A driver with a local coach firm had the habit of dropping off his passengers at the foot of Abergynolwyn station drive with instructions to enjoy the train ride while he, no doubt, went to Wharf for a peaceful cup of tea. We were not given any warning of this and the station staff had the job of issuing separate tickets to upwards of 30 people while the train crew found room for them. Having informed the queue of the single fare to Tywyn, I left the station bloke to get on with the booking while I found seats for the extra passengers; then, with that apprehensive tingling of the spine that heralds the approach of the unexpected, I looked towards the booking office. She was big, and I mean big, in a large black dress that draped from her shoulders right to the ground, and hair that seemed to want to follow suit – I swear blind the wind had dropped and the birds had stopped singing. It transpired that the shape really fitted, as she was a genuine Southern Belle and, as 'Armsinglewardyawanme' was bellowed down the platform, I cringed and was informed by one of her fellow passengers that it was all right for me as they had had the treatment all morning and, with the prospect of the afternoon ahead of them, were not amused.

It had rained fairly steadily during the day, but a bright moonlit evening found three reputedly sane but daring Talyllyn stalwarts, namely David Woodhouse, David Best and myself, concealed in the still and windless woods just above Forestry Crossing on the Extension. On our way up we had dropped off Bill Bishop at Quarry Siding, and in the mystical twilight now awaited the Ghost Train. Reports from farms along the railway that the faint sound of a small internal combustion engine and the steady, rhythmical beat of steel wheel upon steel rail had been heard in the quiet and darkening hours and was causing a certain amount of consternation. Management had brooded over this spiritual phenomenon for many a long candle-lit hour and judged that it was the devilish work of a being that knew the best location for placing its spectral steed upon the sanctified and hallowed rails of the Talyllyn Railway, though the thing had only been heard as the local inhabitants had, presumably, wisely turned their faces to the wall. Thus plans were laid and a trap was set with the three of us cowering in deepening shadows, telephone plugged in and our remote, steadfast and lonely confederate ready to throw over the points to divert the apparition into the empty siding on being given the tip.

We must have lurked for about half an hour when I was overcome not by a chill feeling of impending doom but with a fit of the giggles, and was managerially instructed to be quiet. When I started to giggle again I was asked for the reason and proffered the thought that it was daft that three sound-minded and upright pillars of our exulted Society should be spending a darkening evening on a remote Welsh hillside with rainwater that dripped off the surrounding trees finding its way down our necks, all in the forlorn hope

Volunteers' stories

that we had picked the right night and the right location to apprehend an apparition that may or may not appear, and, besides, I needed a pint. After a moment's reflective pause the giggling became infectious and the surreptitious scheme had to be abandoned, so, with none of us in a fit state to undertake nocturnal ghost-busting, we collected Bill at Quarry and returned to Tywyn and another kind of spirit. Some time later, after it had bounced over the ropes of a party abseiling, with permission, off Dolgoch Viaduct, giving everyone concerned a real fright, it disappeared into the fading light and its ghostly presence passed into Talyllyn legend. There had been two main suspects, but obviously nothing of substance would ever be proved.

David Woodhouse sometimes went up to the Ffestiniog Railway at Porthmadog for marketing meetings with Alan Heywood, and on this occasion had left Dave Best and myself to run Wharf, as was the way of things before Controllers came into being and when whoever was nearest did the job that needed attention. Part way through the day John Thomas, who looked after the museum, entered the office in an excited state and tried to explain that something was wrong. When John became excited he was very difficult to understand, so I went with him to the museum and found a group of foreign visitors in a rather agitated state. It transpired that one of them had dropped an umbrella down the chimney of *Dot*, the little green loco from Beyer Peacock's works, and was anxious to retrieve it. Now, I am more than 6 feet tall, the tallest of the party only came up to my shoulders, and it was quite a stretch for me to reach the top of the chimney, so exactly how one of them had managed to achieve the feat is a mystery that was never explained. The only way of extracting the umbrella was through the smokebox door, which, unfortunately, was secured by a number of bolts and not a central screwed fixing, so we had to wait for the next down train to arrive before we could borrow a spanner. Mike Green made a great play of wielding his adjustable, and when he opened the door it only took a short time to recover the umbrella, which was handed back to its owner while we speculated as to what would have happened if the thing had opened when in the smokebox.

Bryan Green of the permanent staff, and no relation to Mike, brought a long, thin, newspaper-wrapped parcel into the office one day and, after putting it in a corner, asked us to look after it until he came back from his driving trip. The train duly departed and a few minutes later David Ratcliff, the driver of the loco that had brought the train into Wharf, entered the office in very high dudgeon and, walking straight up to the Traffic Manager, announced that some irresponsible person had removed the regulator handle from his locomotive, which could not now be moved. Seeing David's fury and indignation, it seemed prudent not to react, but once the parcel had been handed over and the driver was well on his way back to his immobile steed, the gales of laughter from the office must have been heard all over Wharf station. Next day Bryan was summoned to the loco foreman's office by Herbert Jones and the reprimand he received was tempered by the fact that Herbert had a terrible job trying not to laugh.

Dolgoch and its footbridge was the location for one of Herbert Jones's party tricks, the build-up starting when we rolled into the station with a down train. He would collect some plastic cups from the tables on Aber platform and proceed to fill them with coal dust and oil until he had about half a dozen, then, on being given the 'right away', the regulator was just opened enough to start the train and the cups added to the fire. The footbridge has always been a popular vantage point to watch the departing train, and it was hoped that a number of mini-skirted young ladies would be among the spectators as, when passing under the bridge, the regulator was opened wide, resulting in a volcanic eruption from the chimney and a Welsh cry of 'Dirty knickers!' from the footplate. Nobody ever complained, and the memorial plaque, engraved 'Dirty Knickers H.R.J.', affixed to the under-girders of the footbridge, was removed during the bridge rebuilding, though it still exists on the railway and its reinstatement would be a nice tribute to a great character.

Some time in the late 1960s Joe Storer and I, both in a skittish frame of mind, went to Dolgoch to man the booking office and had dealt with some arrivals and departures when we became conscious that an Army squaddy, who had been sitting dejectedly at the far end of the shelter, had now been joined by a lady. Joe went out to deal with the next up train and after it had arrived I had a fleeting glimpse from the booking office of a tall military figure in knee-length khaki shorts with polished shoes and cine-camera, loping along the platform towards the loco – and when I say 'loping' I am sure that both his feet were off the ground at the same time, which made him bob up and down in a surreal manner. Joe got rid of the train and returned to the office with a huge grin on his face, telling me that he would explain all later. It transpired that he did not have to explain, as a cut-glass, high-pitched voice exclaimed, 'Ohh, the chappies are still har,' and Joe turned so that his back was to the inside of the door and he could not be seen from outside. The postcards on sale were examined by the military presence to the accompaniment of a quiet, tuneless whistling interspersed with some indecipherable muttering, which, I noted, had caused Joe's head to roll back and his mouth to open in a silent laugh. Then, with the postcard perusal complete, the capped and bespectacled head was turned to the waiting shelter and the command 'Miss Jones – pick a card' was issued, the lady eventually responding to the summons.

Joe, still with open mouth, had now slid part way down the door and, as if gold had been found, 'Ohh look – wailway lettah stamps, how delightfully quaint' echoed round the building.

An early photograph of loco No 4 *Edward Thomas* at Dolgoch Falls station. The refreshment van next to the engine will be shunted into the siding at Abergynolwyn on arrival there and taken back to Tywyn at the end of the day. *TR Collection*

This now caused Joe to sit on the floor with his knees up under his chin and a little tear to run down his cheek. Exhaustive examination of the stamps prefaced the unforgettable question delivered in parade-ground fashion to the squaddy: 'Stubbay, does the Brigadeeah collect stamps?' Joe was now rocking gently from side to side, mouth wide open, tears rolling down his cheeks with just the whites of his eyes showing and giving me a demonstration of what can only be described as silent hysterics. It was all right for him being behind the door, but I was on full public view and had to suppress my pent-up laughter, which was becoming painfully difficult. To the same tuneless whistle, stamps and souvenirs were eventually selected and, with a great flourish, a pile of loose change was deposited on the counter accompanied by 'Ohh, take it out of that'. I dutifully 'took it out of that' and, returning the remainder to military custody, received, 'Ohh, look at what I have got back – just like playing Monopoly – bye bye.'

It was some time before we both regained our composure, closed up the office and made our way to the car park, the drive back to Towyn (as it then was) being in a decorous manner. When we walked into the office and 'Traffman' asked us if we had had a good day, the whole episode came flooding back and we both sat on the floor howling with laughter, much to the consternation of management.

Dolgoch Viaduct, wheelbarrows and 'Dizzy' combined in a situation that I would have loved

Volunteers' stories

to have witnessed but had to make do with the revelations of a person present in the pub that evening. It would seem that some lineside work was being undertaken in the cutting at the north-west side of the viaduct, with any material being tipped safely down the slope adjacent to the low parapet wall. All was going well until 'Dizzy' lost control and forgot to let go of the tipping wheelbarrow, at which point it took control. Luckily he got caught in a tree at the very top and was quickly hauled back up, with the barrow now in the stream below. The barrow was collected and the uninjured but dazed 'Dizzy' was informed that as everybody else could handle wheelbarrows correctly he should do the same, but it fell on deaf ears; a while later he did the self same thing again and was relegated to digging as far from the viaduct as possible. Though 'Diz' was a smashing bloke, and always willing to help, this sort of incident was typical of him and you had to be on your guard.

I am sure every blockman on the railway has been at Quarry Siding when it has rained, but on this particular occasion it was throwing it down so hard that sighting the west-end point was becoming difficult and the north side of the valley had totally disappeared. Janet Cox, at Brynglas, had opened up her blockpost and we had a quick discussion over the phone to decide which of us was the wettest after putting out our stop boards. She thought I was 'bloody lucky' as I only had to pass trains without any scheduled crossings, though trips to my west sighting board were going to be damp in the extreme. The rain was hammering on the roof, with thunder about, and I was contemplating using my Bardic lamp to signal the next up train when out of the gloom staggered a hunched and very bedraggled figure. I did not recognise him but was not going outside to investigate as he was already wet enough for both of us and when he arrived at the blockpost door he said he wanted information about volunteering on the railway. I remember thinking Why here?, Why now?, Why not wait until it is just pouring down? I bade him enter and started to answer his questions while leaning on the Brynglas token instrument, when all of a sudden I was thrown across the blockpost to the accompaniment of jangling block bells, though I noted that he hadn't stopped talking and that his eyes had followed my trajectory as if he believed this was a normal occurrence. I was pulling myself together when Jan rang to shakily ask if I was all right as she had had a lightning strike in the field just behind her blockpost and everything had gone mad. I wanted to quickly rid myself of the garrulous stranger and directed him in the direction of Pendre, which must have worked as he staggered off in that general direction.

Finding out that Jan had recovered a bit and that she did not have any trains about, we proceeded to test everything to make sure it all worked, which, thankfully, it did – you know, ding, ding, ding on the block bells, then find out if the token machines still worked. Ding from Jan followed by my reply, then ding, ding, ding pause ding, to request a token. We tried all the procedures laid down in standing orders and

The late Janet Cox was one of the stalwarts of the TR for many years, as a Guard, Controller, Blockman, Booking Clerk and Training Officer. Here she talks to one of the loco crew as No 6 takes water at Dolgoch. As she is not in TR uniform, it must be a special occasion either to celebrate her birthday or her wedding anniversary. The TR is very good at celebrations! *TR Collection*

some that we had devised ourselves over the years and all worked normally for the rest of the shift, though Jan said she could smell what she hoped was sulphur for an hour afterwards. Next day I was recounting the experience down at Wharf and was advised to notify Maurice Wilson, who was top man at that time, of the occurrence as it may have to be recorded in the incident book, so across I went across to see him. Following my knock on the office door I was bidden to enter and Maurice enquired as to what he could do for me.

'Well, Maurice, I don't know ding if you have heard ding what happened at Brynglas ding and Quarry Siding yesterday but I was thrown ding across the blockpost after a lightning ding strike at Brynglas and it has been suggested ding that I should report the ding incident to you in case ding there are any after effects ding.'

He leaned back in his chair while looking at me over the top of his glasses and, after a long pause, said that I appeared to be quite normal and that there was nothing to worry about. I thanked him for his attention, went back outside and roared with laughter at the greatest put-down I have ever experienced. Cheers, Maurice!

In Society days it was very unusual indeed to work a loose-coupled train of passenger stock up the line without a brake-van at the west end, though we managed to do it for a photographic special during a summer in the late 1960s. It had been organised by the British Travel Association for international publicity purposes, and the photographer wanted to use the engine with a lot of bumps on it together with a green coach and that funny brake-van with the sliding doors. No 6, a Glyn and van No 5 were duly organised for the great day, though management were flummoxed when requested to put the van next to the engine with the Glyn behind it, as the last vehicle would then be unbraked. Bill Faulkner and David Woodhouse mused over this precedent for some time, but finally agreed to the request with the proviso that we be extremely careful. David Palmer, Ian Faulkner and Bill Gardner, who were to be the passengers, helped me load some large cardboard boxes into the van just as the principal photographic models arrived. Of him I have little recollection, but Lisa was tall, blonde and Danish and, well, what more can I say, except that she had all the requirements to carry out a first-class job. Dai's jaw dropped nearly to platform level when he first set eyes on her, and after introductions we set off for Rhydyronen where the first batch of photos were to be taken.

On arrival the boxes were found to contain

Rhydyronen in the spring – but this time the daffodils are real! *TR Collection*

Volunteers' stories

Driver Dai Jones, with his son David as his fireman, stands by his favourite engine (No 2 *Dolgoch*) in Pendre Yard on the occasion of his last day as an employee and driver before his retirement in September 1986 on the day of the Society AGM. *TR Collection*

plastic daffodils, which required to be planted around the loco and van to provide a springtime ambience, which seemed out of place in high summer; however, spurred on by a soft Danish accent we satisfactorily completed the task. With Lisa looking out from the fireman's side of the footplate, a grinning Dai tight behind her (lucky so-and-so), Alan Barrett, the fireman, standing on the side of the loco and the rest of us grouped on the platform, pictures were taken from just about every angle until we had to harvest the daffs and run up to Dolgoch for the next session. This part of the trip I found to be rather dull as I was on my own in the van while the rest of them were in very convivial company in the Glyn, though the occasional provocative gesture from Dai when he crossed over to the fireman's side of the footplate showed clearly that he was also in the same frame of mind.

After the loco had taken water we were all positioned to the photographer's satisfaction with the young lady again on the footplate, though his instruction to Dai, the last to pose, of 'OK Dai, get on the job' made the guard and pseudo-passengers nearly fall through the rhododendron bushes. We then went up to Abergynolwyn to be out of the way of the service train and, much to Dai's chagrin, Lisa elected to ride in the brake-van after politely declining a footplate trip back

down the line. Alan said afterwards that every time Dai asked him if he could see me at the van door he untruthfully replied 'No, I haven't seen him since Aber or Quarry or Brynglas,' which brought forth laughter. We stopped at Rhydy for a couple of photos, and she resumed her seat in the Glyn; we all received a smile and a husky thank you upon arrival at Wharf, though she never did return to the railway as an assistant guard. There never has been and never will be another photographic special to remotely match that one.

No 6 will forever be remembered as 'Father's engine', and Hugh's smile as he drove the loco up and down the line must surely be etched in the memories of all who knew him. He had worked either in the quarry or on the railway since the age of 14 and knew all there was to know about the Talyllyn track and locos, though his spirited running with late trains must have taken its toll on both. It took time to get to know Hugh, but to be greeted with a smile and warm handshake at the start of your volunteering stint meant that you had been accepted with an enjoyable time in prospect. He was a great character, and regular visits to Plas Goch to chat about his life on the railway and to hear the other side of the printed stories of the society's early days were at times hilarious and always sincere. I feel privileged to have been a friend and my proudest yet saddest day on the railway was Friday 22 September 1989 when, at the request of his family, I was the guard of the train that conveyed him, in TR van No 5, on his last journey on the railway from Rhydyronen to Pendre.

Recollections of journeys to Tywyn are many, and being introduced to the delights of the extremely pre-Dickensian Fountain Gift Shop in Stratford-upon-Avon and the desolation of 'Tabitha's' in the stygian dark of a Worcestershire night by David Ratcliff and Keith Bannister really added to the fun, though I shall always be puzzled by the Phantom Hitch Hiker of Ludlow.

Tony McIllwrick

In his childhood, in the late 1920s, my father had travelled on the TR when on holiday with his parents and sister, and in due course he and my mother introduced me to the TR in the late 1940s and early 1950s during a series of holidays that we spent at Fairbourne. Three photographs of me at Abergynolwyn taken in the summer of 1950 in an album belonging to my father attest to this. We continued to visit the TR periodically during the next 15 years; two of my earliest memories from this period are of the reconstruction of the road bridge at Wharf and of the building of the north carriage shed.

As a student in the four-year period 1965-68 my timetable permitted almost no holidays because I was doing a 'sandwich' course that

The approach to Wharf Station as it was in 1965. TR Collection

Volunteers' stories

meant being in college in Sheffield from January to June, then industrial work from July to December each year. In fact, apart from a few days at Christmas and the New Year my only entitlement was a fortnight each Easter.

I felt the need for a holiday, but as a student it had to be inexpensive and I think that it was my mother who, in an inspired move, suggested that a working holiday at Easter on either the Talyllyn or the Festiniog might meet my requirements, each being well known to me.

I therefore wrote to the Chief Engineers of both organisations and received a very welcoming reply from John Bate, Chief Engineer of the TR (in complete contrast to the very unwelcoming letter that I received from the FR), and set off at Easter 1965. The TR had sent me a list of accommodation and I had chosen a farmhouse some miles outside the town at Tynllwynhen. Landlady Mrs Humphries was an elderly Welsh-speaking widow and had sold or leased the farmland following the death of her husband but retained her home at the end of a long, rough farm track.

I thoroughly enjoyed myself during that first working visit to the TR, for although I have no precise recollection of what I did in that first year I worked outside, spending most of the time on track work with Geoff Hayes – re-sleepering along Wharf edge, in the yard at Pendre and along Ty Mawr embankment with people who made me very welcome and appeared to value my contribution, however modest. I returned home hooked and have been an enthusiastic participant ever since.

My second visit, at Easter 1966, coincided with very poor weather. I was first detailed to join the gang digging ballast at the TR quarry while snow fell, an unpleasant task that did nothing to diminish my enthusiasm. Then on one particularly wet and really unpleasant day, Easter Sunday, 10 April, I was asked to assist TRPS Secretary Richard Hope. Some time in the mid-1960s the cutting between Wharf and Pendre stations developed drainage problems and subsequently a small landslide occurred. John Bate designed a scheme to overcome the problems – a new drain along the length of the cutting and a U-shaped steel frame that went underneath the track and with vertical struts that restrained the sides of the cutting from slipping down again onto the track. This frame was made out of lengths of scrap rail welded together on site. The entire project of drain and frame construction took some considerable time and effort to build; Richard was doing some welding on the framework and needed an assistant – me. The working conditions were atrocious for the cutting was very wet, we were ankle deep in glutinous mud and it was raining hard. We were using a diesel-powered welding set and the noise of this made communication between us almost impossible unless we were just a few inches apart. While my back was turned Richard slipped and found himself attached to the U frame by the electrical current. With my back to him his shouts of alarm were of no use as I could not hear him until eventually I turned round and saw his predicament, and turned off the generator engine to enable his release. It was a salutary lesson in the dangers of undertaking such tasks in very bad working conditions. I also spent time pouring concrete for the foundations of Brynglas blockpost and for a new building behind the north carriage shed.

A third visit, two years later at Easter 1968, saw me entrusted by John Bate with the installation at the entrance to Wharf station of a gatepost. Manufactured out of steel, it sat in a steel sleeve concreted into the ground so that, after removal of the gate and the adjacent fencing, it could easily be lifted out to allow access by large vehicles. In order to carry out this task I got to use a pneumatic breaker and a concrete mixer (realising in each case a childhood ambition to use such machines), finding that the former in particular was very hard work. I also spent some time working on the conversion of the cottage at Pendre into an enlargement of the engine shed; I spent several days building up the wall above the door into the works, having previously cast a concrete lintel in situ. After this I returned to Wharf to work on re-gauging the curved track that leads to the Wharf edge as well as helping to unload a new carriage body from the delivery lorry that had brought it from the Midlands.

All this wide variety of tasks has led me to spend the intervening years on various outdoor programmes of which the most recent and deeply satisfying is working, as part of a team of six volunteers, on the construction of a weighbridge building at Wharf.

John Scott

The past, when you could have a three-course meal at the Ritz, see a major London show, get a taxi home and still have change from sixpence, etc, is I time I don't remember. My avid trainspotting days were much later, when steam was still common on the main line and 'cabbing' a 'Britannia' at Blackpool South was a regular event on the way home from school.

Around this time my family had two holidays in Wales. The first was in North Wales and we visited the Snowdon and Festiniog railways. When we arrived at the FR it seems that the train had broken down so we never actually travelled on it and the FR lost an opportunity for a new volunteer, from which I hope it has recovered. However, in 1965 we visited Mid Wales and travelled on the Vale of Rheidol and the TR.

For a 12-year-old the TR was spectacular. First, it seemed to have lots of children working on it. Second, when about to depart on the return journey from Abergynolwyn my parents could not find me as I had disappeared up the Extension. I soon returned but the guard had actually held the train for me. This had to be the railway to work on, although I had to wait two more years to be old enough.

John Scott. *John Scott collection*

In 1967 I joined the Loco Department for my first week's volunteering. My parents had rather rashly agreed to lend out their pristine touring caravan to me and two friends to use on our own. Before they left my father delivered me to Wharf from where Tris England sent me to Pendre to report to Herbert Jones. At this time the main running shed only held two engines as the internal wall of Herbert's cottage was still there, so other engines were either outside or in a carriage shed. One of my first jobs involved going back to Wharf to fill a hopper wagon, in the course of which I sustained my first railway injury when my head came into contact with the edge of the wagon. I still have the scar on my head and the bloodstain on my original greasetop hat. I think my first loco cleaning job was on No 1. It then had a brass-plated dome, which seemed to take for ever to clean so was not favoured by the cleaners. Keeping yourself clean was also not so easy as Pendre had one toilet and a sink in the washroom. Still, as a young cleaner getting dirty was half the fun. The caravan did not look so pristine at the end of the week.

I had heard about things called 'third man' trips, but these seemed to be only a rumour as no one seemed to be having them. As the week went by I was more and more desperate to get a trip on an engine so in a bold move I decided to ask Herbert Jones if this might be possible. He must have thought I had been of some use during the week, so diplomatically said that if the driver did not mind I could have a trip on No 6 at the end of the week. The driver of No 6 was the legendary Hugh Jones, and the fireman was the equally legendary Roy Smith. The trip was just fantastic. It all looked so easy and well-organised and the crew patiently explained to me how it all worked. On arrival at Abergynolwyn I was amazed to be offered my own free personal cup of tea by the guard John Gott, which at the time was served from the Tea Van in the little siding. All this was more than enough to make me return for another season. One week was clearly not long enough, so subsequent visits were for at least two.

In 1968 I first met David Ratcliff, who was a senior fireman and subsequently one of the newly

Volunteers' stories

John with No 6 in the yard at Pendre. *John Scott collection*

promoted volunteer drivers, together with Roy Smith. David took on the responsibility of getting the cleaners properly trained while I was there and we had the first of the 'training trains', which the cleaners fired and David drove. The engine for the first one was No 4, with its Giesl ejector. I believe we had a simulated 'passenger falling out of the train' incident as part of the trip, involving, I think, a stuffed body. Although our firing experience was minimal, we now understood at lot more about running trains and cleaning engines and David was an excellent teacher. Third man trips were now much more the norm and my first firing trip came about because an extra train was put on at the end of the day, so the firemen got off and I took over. It was No 3 (still in grey primer) with Herbert driving. Well, we got there and back, fortunately, with the odd word of advice from Herbert who had that instinct for what was happening in the firebox. I was on my way to becoming a fireman.

Pranks and incidents of various kinds were

John cleaning No 6's regulator lubricator in the shed before starting the day's trips up and down the line. *John Scott collection*

more common then than now (probably just as well), and wiring up the firehole door to stop the firemen opening it at light-up, stuffing things down chimneys and heating the train staff when on the line did occur. Displays of smoke or worse were caused by plastic cups of cylinder oil (and sand) added to the fire – by the drivers, I hasten to add. A more innocent prank was to make a brisk start with a view to leaving the assistant guard behind. This happened one evening at Brynglas with Herbert driving, and the poor assistant walked all the way to Dolgoch to rejoin the down train. I don't know why the guard did not stop the train. Another interesting event used to be the train occasionally splitting in half when pulling away from Brynglas due to our somewhat strange combination of couplings and buffers at that time. One fireman managed to lose his shovel and was reduced to literally hand firing, and another, in a misguided economy drive, actually ran out of coal and had to survive on scraps of wood from the lineside.

Firing trips that go badly are always more useful than incident-free ones, since if you can recover the situation it is a valuable learning exercise. On one of my early trips on No 4 with David Ratcliff driving we decided to use a very thin fire to see if we could get a very economical trip. It was before the Extension opened and we therefore ran round at Abergynolwyn and went for our tea break. Unfortunately we had neglected to look at the fire, as we were so pleased with our economical run. On returning to the engine everything seemed ominously quiet. A look in the firebox revealed a few glowing embers. Help, I thought, it will be the end of my short

Volunteers' stories

career! David was not perturbed and, following his advice of little bits of coal and a squirt or two of lubricating oil as we went down the line, everything was back to normal by Pendre and nobody was any the wiser. As a driver I have had this happen to my fireman and I can be equally imperturbable now.

A not very popular job for cleaners was emptying a main-line 20-ton coal wagon at Wharf; we also used to screen the coal to remove the slack, a little pile of which used to be left at the Wharf platform buffer stops for use if you were short of fire to get back to Pendre with the empty stock. The coal then was the legendary South Wales variety such as Lady Windsor, which gave rise to a short-lived jazz band on the TR known as Lady Windsor and her Cobbles, led by Henry Davies. Musical interludes have always been a feature for me on the TR, and from fairly early on I played trombone for Tywyn Silver Band. We even once took a jazz band complete with piano on a Boflat up to Dolgoch for a party.

When I finished school I went to university to study Engineering Science, and was able to spend more time in the summer on the TR and contribute more to the engineering side of the railway. When I was 21 Herbert sprang on me the news that if I could put in an extra week I would get some driver training. Needless to say I fixed the extra week. At the time the TR's MD was not overly keen on having volunteer drivers, but as his own health got worse he realised the benefit of having someone to take over his turns and eventually the day of my first solo driving trip arrived. It was a wet evening and the loco was No 6, the engine on which I had first had a footplate trip back in 1967. I had no need to worry about the firing as Malcolm Brown, a future driver, was on that side and it all seemed to go pretty well. No 6 is still my favourite engine, and the TR my favourite railway. It has occupied a large part of my life and I have met and worked with lots of wonderful people. To be part of such a historic enterprise has been an honour.

John Burton

I first visited the Talyllyn Railway in May 1966 with my parents and sister. We stayed at the camp site at Tynllwyn, which was then just a farmer's field, with little to show that it was a camping and caravan site. I remember the guard on the first Talyllyn train we travelled on, later to be identified as one John Smallwood, whom I was to come to know very well.

The week was spent travelling around to the Ffestiniog, Welshpool & Llanfair, Vale of Rheidol and Fairbourne railways. I did, though, have a day travelling up and down on all the three TR trains that were running that day. I also remember spending a morning 'Brassoing' carriage door handles in Pendre yard.

The following year I volunteered as a cleaner in the Locomotive Department. I was just 12 – there was no minimum age of 14 in those days.

John Burton. *Terry Gurd*

The locomotive shed only held two locos at that time; it had not yet been extended into the former cottage. A memory from the first day is of a fireman filling the shed with smoke lighting up *Talyllyn*; there was no air line to attach to the blower in those days. I also remember having to polish *Talyllyn*'s brass dome before it was painted over (the brass was only a sprayed-on coating). Much of that week was spent drying sand for locomotive use on an improvised drier alongside the back road. Another memory from this week was the Corris van being used in passenger service, as Van 10 was out of service pending the fitting of a new body, and Van 5 was also undergoing major repairs.

The following year, 1968, I had my first 'third man' trip, on *Talyllyn*, with Herbert Jones and Bryan Green. It then becomes difficult to remember individual weeks of cleaning. I do remember, though, that although I had many third man trips, they were all as spectator; it was not the practice to give the cleaner the shovel as happens today. And it was certainly not the done thing for the cleaner to ask to have a chance with the shovel – as I discovered! I only had one trip firing under supervision. That was in 1971, on *Dolgoch* with Herbert Jones and Tony Leaver. I must have done reasonably well because Herbert gave me a passed cleaner's grade card on the strength of it.

All this time I had been staying with the rest of the family at Tynllwyn. For someone who couldn't yet drive, this did present some difficulties getting to and from Pendre. Often it meant getting father to deliver and collect me. However, on occasions it was possible to get a lift home with Hugh Jones, who lived in the cottage 'Plas Coch' opposite Rhydyronen station. He used to commute to and from Pendre using the PW trolley, which was kept overnight in the siding where the west end of the platform is now. On other occasions, particularly when going in for early turns, it was possible to get a lift from

Driver Roy Smith is ready to exchange the Wharf-Pendre token for the Pendre-Brynglas token with the Pendre Blockman as No 1 *Talyllyn* heads the Vintage Train through Pendre Yard. *TR Collection*

Volunteers' stories

Roy Smith, who used to stay in the farmhouse at Tynllwyn.

On my next visit, in 1972, I was surprised to find I had been given a full week of firing, on *Edward Thomas*, *Douglas* and *Sir Haydn* with Bill Faulkner, Hugh Jones and David Ratcliff, all sadly now deceased.

Promotion to Fireman came in 1976, then a long wait until 2001 for promotion to Passed Fireman, and finally to Driver in 2009.

There were incidents. One of them in the 'now it can be told' category is the time when, firing for Bill Faulkner, we arrived at Nant Gwernol without the all-important staff, which meant that we couldn't unlock the points to run the engine round the train. This was largely my fault, but Bill should have checked. I was sent back down the track to collect the staff, while Ed Lund, station master at Abergynolwyn, set off up the line with it – we met at about Forestry Crossing.

On another occasion we were held at Abergynolwyn because the previous train had lost the staff en route; it had fallen off *Douglas* without the crew noticing. Eventually we were able to proceed under the authority of a pilotman (John Smallwood). Later, after a search involving a number of people, the staff was found and normal service could be resumed the following day.

My career in the Traffic Department has been rather less than conventional. I can honestly say that I have never done a day as a trainee in that department, even though I am qualified for all, or nearly all, of the jobs. This is something that would not be possible today with the current emphasis on training and assessment.

The first job I did for the Traffic Department

> **Quite often a party of photographers spends three days or so, out of season, taking photos of TR trains in many locations on the line. The train stops to let the photographers disembark and get into position, then does as many 'run pasts' as the photographers need to get the shots they want. They then board the train and it moves on to the next chosen location. On 18 March 2006 such a train stands at Wharf station, headed by No 2 *Dolgoch*. John Burton is driving and Nigel Adams is the Guard, seen standing by the corner of the building. Two other volunteers, Dave Pegg and Bob Hey, are talking on the platform.** *Chris Worley, TR Collection*

was that of blockman. This came about because when the three-set service was introduced in 1969, with crossing of trains at Pendre and Quarry Siding as well as Brynglas (Abergynolwyn was the terminus at that time), the job of Pendre blockman was a turn for a spare cleaner. This may be connected with the fact that there wasn't a blockpost at Pendre at this time, and there were two groundframes, so that the blockman had to walk the length of the loop to operate the points. His shelter was the locomotive shed where the block instruments lived in the alcove that currently houses the loco shed telephones. No training was given – you worked it all out as you went along. When the blockpost was built, and the new frame installed that could control both ends of the loop, the job of Pendre blockman was taken over by the Traffic Department. However, I was able to convince the Traffic Manager that I knew the basics of blocking, and to continue as a blockman all I had to do was learn how to keep the block register, as no register was kept at Pendre during the time the Loco Department ran it.

During June 1984 my parents arranged to rent a caravan at Tynllwyn for a fortnight, and told me I was welcome to join them if I wanted. I was able to get some time off work, so I called Wharf to find out whether volunteers were needed during that time. The fortnight spanned a week of single-set services and a week of two-set services, and I thought a blockman might be needed for the latter. However, that week wasn't a problem – what was a problem was the previous week, as there were no guards, and in those days there were no local volunteers to fill in on such occasions. I told David Woodhouse I was prepared to give it a try if he was, so I drove down on the Wednesday morning to find the set sitting in the platform at Wharf, where it had been left the previous evening so that the Wharf cleaner could sweep it out. David Woodhouse and Phil Care had shared the job for the previous two days, but this day I was out on my own for the first time. I don't remember any particular incidents, but I do remember that things became more complicated the following day when I had an assistant rostered! So it went on until the weekend.

On the Saturday the traffic was quite busy, and I remember a particularly hectic time at Dolgoch on the first down journey. A group of young people came up to me and said they were getting off the train, having travelled down from Nant Gwernol, and did I want them to pay their fare? They gave me a £50 note, hoping, I think, that I would say that I couldn't change it and let them off. However, I had been doing good business in the van and by pooling nearly all of the contents of the cash box I was just about able to change the note; I handed over a great pile of loose change with the tickets, and their faces fell. Then, of course, there was a full train of tickets to clip. Fortunately for me, the driver was Colin Roobottom, who could see how busy I was and volunteered to go and clip the train for me. Since then, when working on the locomotive and seeing a hard-pressed guard, I have on occasions gone and helped him with the clipping, which sometimes amuses the passengers. On the strength of those few days' work David Woodhouse was kind enough to issue me with a guard's grade card.

While David Woodhouse was Traffic Manager, and later General Manager, he played a major part in controlling the operation of the railway. When he left the situation changed, and volunteer controllers had to be rostered, with full responsibility for operation. The controllers were drawn mainly from the ranks of the blockmen. I booked as available for traffic duties on the following Spring Bank Holiday weekend, and was surprised to find that I had been rostered as Controller on the Bank Holiday Sunday. I can therefore claim to be the first person to have had to control a full three-set service in the post-Woodhouse era. It was quite an experience! For one thing there were no published set formations. On the previous day there had been two sets in service, and these formed the first two trains, but when the third guard came into the office and asked, 'What do you want me to bring down?' I had to try and remember what was on the other two sets and what would be left behind. I said something like, 'Leave an open and a TR and bring the rest.' At the appointed time the train appeared under Wharf road bridge, and more and more coaches appeared until the whole train was in the platform. The next thing I knew was the driver rushing into the office to use the phone and summon a diesel from Pendre because the length of the train had blocked the loop and he couldn't run round! Needless to say punctuality was not very good that day.

Then there is the engineering work. For many years I have done this for the railway, particularly outside the running season. I gravitated towards

Volunteers' stories

carriage work, eventually becoming Carriage Foreman. One day during the running season I was carrying out some repairs to the roof of carriage No 22 in the West Carriage Shed. At lunchtime, as usual, I walked down to Wharf for lunch, leaving my tools on the roof of the coach, ready to resume after lunch. However, as I finished lunch and prepared to walk back to Pendre, it became obvious that a crisis was developing. *Talyllyn* had failed at Abergynolwyn, and engine and train were going to have to be rescued. I was given the keys to Abergynolwyn blockpost and dispatched up the valley in the car to assist with the rescue. The delay that the failure had caused meant that the train would not be back at Wharf for its next working, so a scratch set had to be assembled and this duly left Wharf behind a hastily steamed *Douglas*. As it arrived at Abergynolwyn I was a little concerned to see No 22 on the back of the train. Fortunately there was a ladder in the blockpost and I was able to climb up and recover my tools, which had all survived the journey. In an ironic twist, I was at the centre of another similar incident some years later when, as driver, *Sir Haydn* failed on me in almost exactly the same place and we, in turn, had to be rescued.

Richard Wood

A notice appeared in the local paper about a Talyllyn Railway Meeting to be held on 25 February 1967 in a pub on Ashbourne Road in Derby. As I had not had much to do with the TR for a good number of years, I went along, and met for the first time Donald Heath who, at that time, was working in the Railway Research Centre in Derby. He used to drive to Towyn for a day's work on the railway, and soon after meeting him I joined him on these trips. As a result of the meeting our day trips to Towyn attracted quite a following, and Donald became the East Midlands Working Party Organiser. We had a very loyal group and sadly I can now only remember a few names: Nick Potter, Arthur Cushway, Ed Lund, Chris White and later Don Newing. In due course Donald moved to Rugby and I took over as the Working Party organiser. I suppose these day trips to Towyn would not be feasible today, but then there was no problem.

Memories of the East Midlands Working Parties, 1967-75. This is laying Fach Goch siding in 1970.

We left Derby at 6.00am and called at Welshpool for a comfort stop, where, incidentally, the local staff kept the copper and brass extremely well polished. Arriving at Pendre between 9.00 and 9.30, we then got a good day's work done, and I soon learned never to be separated from my picnic lunch. I usually started with oxtail soup and finished with a can of beer; the latter I imagine would not be allowed today due to stringent Health & Safety rules. Leaving Pendre at dusk, we called for an all-day breakfast at the Milk Bar in Welshpool, getting back to Derby at 10.00pm. Petrol cost was not a problem – £1 from each passenger covered the cost, and I collected sufficient Green Shield stamps over the years to claim an aluminium ladder.

Quite often we would have more than one car making the trip. John Bate knew when we were coming so always planned a full day's work for us. More often than not we were out on the track, which I always found most satisfying. There is something elemental in working on the foundations of a railway. Our first major job in April 1970 was laying the initial lengths of track for the Fach Goch siding. The points (or turnouts!) had already been put in and we managed to lay two lengths. During the life of the siding we spent many hours extending and slewing the track across as the hole was gradually being filled up; one got used to seeing *Midlander* leaning over at drunken angles on the siding. I suppose the climax of our efforts was to participate, during the summer of 1971, in the record-breaking number of tipper wagons that were emptied in one day. Several days were spent up on the Extension cutting back the side of the cutting and clearing slate away after blasting.

November 1972 saw us working on track renewal at Six Bends beyond Brynglas. Here, for the first time, all new materials, including rails, were being used. It was on a trip back to Pendre in February 1973 after work up the line with much rain that the cement mixer fell off its wagon and derailed two wagons in the process. I think we had to get some help before the train was able to proceed. Over the winter of 1973/74 our working parties were concentrated on the track between Dolgoch and Quarry Siding. Here we were digging out the old ballast and getting the site ready for relaying work. Later on in the year the draining of Tadpole Cutting required attention. We went up the line complete with an air compressor and pneumatic drill, the job being to deepen the drainage channel. I think that it was the first time any of us had used such a device and it was quite an experience – it certainly increased our admiration for men who had to use them every day. A very smelly job was carried out at Cynfal road bridge where we had to clear the mud off the road prior to the TR resurfacing with tarmac.

My final working parties saw us preparing for a big bang on the Extension, re-ballasting at Fach Goch and starting to lay a new siding at Abergynolwyn. By then the family were growing up, so I had to curtail my outside activities. The working parties had been most enjoyable and fun, working as a team. Quite often John Bate would come and see how we were getting on. They were wonderful days up the valley – we never seemed to have a lot of rain. I was pleased to be able to contribute in a small way to the improvement and maintenance of the Talyllyn Railway.

Volunteers' stories

Oh dear…!

Tipping wagons at Fach Goch.

Tipping used ballast near Dolgoch.

Track work near Dolgoch.

Volunteers' stories

Drilling in Tadpole Cutting, 1974.

Siding work at Abergynolwyn.

Gareth Jones. *Margaret Jones*

Gareth Jones

I joined the Society in 1968 and first volunteered in July of that year as one of a group of four schoolboys from Hull, just out of fifth form. Our group included John Hague, who has written his own account of that first week, which matches very closely my own recollection. I do recall that it was John and I who plucked up courage to ask Herbert Jones for a 'third man' trip at the end of that week, as none appeared to be 'on offer'; my trip was on No 2, with Herbert driving and an equally youthful Chris Parrott firing. We all proudly received our cleaner's cards at the end of that week.

On the train journey back to Hull, on Saturday 3 August, we had to change at Crewe, and picking up a local newspaper we noticed a short piece tucked away in the middle pages, stating that that very evening the last 'proper' steam trains on British Railways were running, both evening departures from Preston. Too good an opportunity to miss, I diverted north, 'bashing' a lifeless Bolton shed full of dead 'Black Fives' and 'Big 8s' on the way. Preston station was heaving with 'gricers', and after the departure of the 20.50 to Blackpool behind No 45212 I caught the very last 'ordinary' steam-hauled passenger train on BR, the 21.25 to Liverpool Exchange behind No 45318, a number forever etched in my memory. After spending the night in a waiting room on Manchester Exchange, the following day was spent watching the passage of the various 'last day specials' (the famous 'Fifteen Guinea Special' followed on 15 August), before finding my way to Lostock Hall depot to watch the very last locos coming on shed and dropping their fires for the last time. All very emotional!

With that door firmly closed, and a new 'steam' interest fired up, we returned to the TR the following year, with two additions, making a group of six. I'm sure in those days you weren't rostered for a particular cleaning turn and I recall that we'd all get up at the crack of dawn and 'blitz' all the locos together. This must have impressed Herbert, because third man trips with firing tuition became the norm that summer, and I graduated through the footplate ranks, eventually becoming a Passed Fireman in 1990, and Driver a few years later.

A few incidents on the footplate stand out in my memory. Prior to the introduction of electric

> This is what can happens when volunteers meet on the TR! Driver Gareth Jones met his wife Margaret (née Walker), who was an Assistant Guard, and they have two children, Neil and Sian. Neil is now a Fireman and Blockman and Sian volunteered in the Traffic Department. Margaret no longer guards trains but is Secretary to one of the Council Committees. *Gareth Jones collection*

Volunteers' stories

Dedication! These five volunteers are celebrating 40 years of volunteering on the TR with a special train and a party. From left to right they are Driver Paul Shuttleworth, Driver Gareth Jones, Fireman (and Guard and Blockman) Dale Coton, Outdoor volunteer Rod Hannah, and Fireman and Outdoor volunteer John Hague. *John Hague collection*

key token single-line working up the line, in 1970 I think, there was what I recall to be a most bizarre system of metal staff and tickets. Their appearance meant that they quickly became known as 'Christmas Trees'. These were huge and heavy lumps, for which there was little room on the loco, so they got piled into any corner of the fireman's side of the cab. During one trip we were distracted by a rather talkative young cleaner, and overcarried the Pendre-Brynglas ingots. We only realised the mistake in Dolgoch Woods, so at the water stop the cleaner was firmly blamed for distracting us, and he was sent to walk back down the track to Brynglas with an armful of what was soon to become scrap metal. I can't possibly divulge the identity of the crew of course ... but as a clue the cleaner subsequently found double-barrelled fame on the high seas, while the driver was a pioneer wearer of a 'baseball' cap and wore light blue overalls with ICI written on them!

In the early 1980s, in the woods around Dolgoch, there was a 'plague' of caterpillars, which kept falling out of the trees and getting squashed on the railhead, making a very slippery surface. I recall approaching Dolgoch on a down train, with Bill Faulkner driving, when his brake application simply had no effect whatsoever, and we just slid all the way through the station and over the viaduct before finally stopping (and sheepishly propelling back to the platform). A case of the wrong type of larvae, rather than the wrong type of leaves, I guess!

In late October 1990, in what turned out to be my last trip as a fireman, I was driving the down afternoon train on No 1, under Phil Guest's supervision, when, approaching the reverse curves at the bottom of Cynfal, I glimpsed something 'different' around Fach Goch, something not quite right – a chap by the fence was it? In anticipation I applied the steam brake (no air brake then) and as the crossing came into view we saw to our horror a large caravan parked firmly across the track, with two guys just standing back watching, seemingly just waiting for the inevitable impact! The TR's guardian angel must have been watching us that day, as unusually, for that second trip of the day, we had an extra brake van on (No 5) to carry some cycles, so three bips on the train alarm and an alert response from the two guards got double braking power, plus the steam brake, and we managed to stop just a few yards short of the obstruction. The van was being towed up to the farm by a tractor and had got stuck against the railhead, but why on earth those chaps just stood there without making any attempt to warn us is still beyond me!

Back in 1969 I'd been on a down train with Hugh Jones on No 6 (handbrake only then, I think!) when we hit a car on Brynglas crossing (the car's fault). In 2000, on a trip to Poland for their standard gauge main-line driving experience (with John Hague), I was driving an OL49 when we hit a transit van that had broken down on a level crossing, and completely demolished it! Luckily there were no injuries, but again people were just standing back watching (their fault) and waiting for the crash!

Two other incidents followed shortly. The first was an unforgettable experience, again on No 6, on a down photographers' special when the radius rod sheared (*Douglas*'s fault!). I'll never forget the look on fireman Martin Fuller's face as he yelled to me to 'Stop!'. Then, when I was helping out at the NRM at Anthony Coulls's invitation on the museum's demonstration line driving the replica Penydarren Tramway loco, an axle sheared (faulty steel) and a driving wheel literally fell off! The loco tipped to one side and I nearly went with it! A number of TR friends were also taking part, and others witnessed this; I believe there's video footage lurking somewhere.

I must assure you that none of these events of course had anything to do with the competence of my driving – I just happened to be in the wrong place at the wrong time! But they nevertheless earned me the only 'Mr Jinxed' Award ever bestowed at the annual pre-New Year Young (?) Members dinner a few years ago.

Ah, memories, memories, so many good times, so many fantastic experiences and good friends. And the thing is, it still goes on, after more than 40 years!

Of course, volunteering encompasses many different disciplines. In 1998 Maurice Wilson approached me in the shed one morning and asked if I'd consider standing for Council. I did, scraped through the ballot, and have served on Council and various committees ever since, eventually being elected onto the Board. So these days I don't seem to spend as much time at Pendre as I'd wish, Council and Board duties taking a lot of my time, but I still try to get in my fair share on the footplate. I help out on outdoor and other duties as and when I can, and it makes a great change from the administrative side of things.

My son Neil and wife Margaret both volunteer in different ways, so it's a real family thing, and whenever we come to Tywyn there are always friends, and a young or old face (not Margaret's) or two to natter to; in fact, we could simply plonk ourselves on a bench outside Wharf cafe on a sunny summer's day and spend the whole time chatting to folk and friends, if not just taking in the atmosphere of such a pleasant place to be!

The TR truly is a family and a community; it transcends age and any other distinctions, and I'm privileged to have spent such a large part of my life as a member. Hopefully, I'll carry on until I drop!

John Hague

To look back over 42 years of being actively involved with the Talyllyn Railway is to look back at the equivalent of a working life, albeit with just a few weeks' involvement each year. It just shows how the TR becomes such a large part of many volunteers' lives.

As schoolboys in the late 1960s a group of us had enjoyed watching steam in action on BR until its demise in 1968 and earlier in that year we had turned our attention to industrial steam, mainly at the coal mines in Yorkshire. Somehow our thoughts moved to the idea of being actively involved with steam. Standard gauge steam preservation was in its infancy, so our attention turned to the Welsh narrow gauge. Fortunately, our parents were accepting of the concept of

Volunteers' stories

John Hague.

four 15-year-old boys going away for a week, unaccompanied, to Wales. My father wrote to the various lines and the most welcoming response came from the TR.

So, come July, it was a train trip from Hull to Leeds where the four of us picked up the York to Aberystwyth Mail for an overnight trip to Wales. This was quite an adventure for the time, when travel was not so extensive as today. After a trip on the Vale of Rheidol line, we progressed to Tywyn for a trip on the TR. Exhaustion then stepped in and, fast asleep at our digs by early evening, we missed the evening meal when it was being served, our landlady thinking we were out.

With our interest in steam, we spent most of the week cleaning locos, and a couple of us obtained 'third man' trips, which were not so readily given in those days. Also, we had a day helping on the track to see something else of the railway. The week quickly passed and what a shock it was to return home for the rest of the school holidays. I had just wanted to stay at Tywyn, having enjoyed the week so much. It was the heady mix of actually being involved with steam rather than just watching, together with the beautiful Welsh countryside and being able to have a degree of independence at a relatively

early age. The trips up the valley on the TR and along the Cambrian Coast from Dovey Junction to Tywyn became sights that I still never fail to enjoy.

So the time passed by with yearly visits and a fairly quick progression to Fireman in 1972 was achieved. The four of us became six in 1969, but today only Gareth Jones and I are still involved with the TR, the others having other interests and commitments. Memories of those early days tend to merge, so it is difficult to recall many detailed events, but a few can be recounted. These were the days of the Jones family on the footplate, together with Bill Faulkner. Herbert, Dai and Hugh were all so kindly and helpful to new volunteers, especially once you had shown your commitment. I remember a very early solo firing trip on No 3 with Herbert, blowing off from time to time as I had yet to master the middle way between over- and under-firing. He did not complain but just said it would all fall into place with time. Dai had his own gentle way of teaching and checking all was in hand without putting one off or putting one down. Hugh, with his ear-to-ear smile on No 6, was always a pleasure to fire for and always amazed me in his acceptance of youngsters from a different time and place from his native Wales. Even Bill, who many feared, caused me no real trouble as long as you did things the way he liked. In the days when driving was the preserve of Bill and the rest of the staff, I remember him letting me propel the stock back to Pendre at the end of one day's operating, which was a great thrill and experience.

The locos in the late 1960s had yet to be rebuilt to today's standards, so firing was a little more demanding than today. No 2 in particular required careful handling and one had to have a hot fire, full glass and be blowing of at Wharf to have any chance of a good trip. This was all part of the TR atmosphere of the time, with more of a sense of adventure than today, heavily loaded trains in the peak and perhaps a more fluid way of operating. Visions come to mind of late-afternoon trains arriving at Dolgoch on the way to Tywyn and we would wonder where to put all the passengers. However, memories depend on the eyes of the viewer and those of a teenager may not be quite the same as one in his late 50s today.

One trip that does remain in mind is a morning trip with Herbert Jones on No 4. Coming into Pendre from Wharf, I looked in the firebox to see water pouring in and showed this to Herbert. A quick loco change took place, and we headed up the valley with diesel No 9, trying to not lose too much time what with the engine being quite slow. On the down trip, coasting out of gear was on many parts of the line quicker than using top gear. For a youngster it was the sheer fun of such trips that stay in the mind.

So to the effect the TR had on my other life. Attempts to obtain an engineering career in BR were not fulfilled, even though I managed the shortlist for an undergraduate training scheme. However, the TR confirmed my interest in engineering, and rather than mechanical engineering, as first intended, I eventually became a Chartered Civil Engineer working in highway maintenance. The time on the TR as a youngster definitely encouraged the taking of responsibility and a work ethic, which proved useful in my career, whether it was being responsible for construction work, running snowploughs in wintry conditions or just dealing with a complete mix of people on a day-to-day basis.

Unfortunately, a prolonged illness for some years prevented my visits to the TR for a time and curtailed my professional career. Bed-bound for some of this time, I would hold in mind the image of Talyllyn Lake looking silvery in the western sun when viewed from the pass. This kept my determination to return to the TR once I recovered. Fortunately, I am now back on the footplate, which is as enjoyable as ever. Also, for some time I have been actively involved in Outdoor Weeks, which has given me the chance to both gain new skills and also use my existing skills. I do like the sense of achievement this gives, especially learning new skills. Just as importantly, I find this and footplate work great fun and very enjoyable, as much as in my early days, but in a slightly different way. Again, is this just the boy becoming the man, or do our freedoms and enjoyments change in different eras?

Finally, the personal side of one's life is affected by the TR. My wife to be, Ruth, was a regular volunteer before we had our boys. We now have a week's family holiday each year staying near the line, enjoying walking in the area, riding on the TR and exploring this beautiful part of Wales. The TR has also become a second family. I have made so many friends and enjoyed many a good conversation both while working on the TR and socially at the end of the day. For those over whom the TR casts its spell, it is magic indeed.

Herbert Jones is fondly remembered by John, and was an employee of the TR until his untimely early death. He had lived in the house that is now part of Pendre loco shed, and after his death a plaque was erected to mark his long service to the railway. Here his family stands in front of the plaque after it had been unveiled in 1984. *TR Collection*

Volunteers' stories

Ian Evans

As a family we holidayed in mid-Wales on several occasions in the 1960s, camping at Cefn Crib (Pennal), Ty'n-y-maes (at the east end of Talyllyn Lake) and later at Gwastadfryn at Llanfihangel y pennant. We travelled on the Festiniog, Rheidol

Ian Evans.

Volunteers' stories

and Talyllyn railways, and Mum tells me that I always made a bee-line for the opens – when they were truly opens and we got covered in smuts!

I joined the Talyllyn Railway Preservation Society at the end of 1968 and very soon reported to Wharf for work. Eric Gibbons's remark that Ian and Evans was an unusual mix of Scottish and Welsh has gone down in family folklore! The following morning I reported to Bob Lee at Pendre, who became the first of many dear friends that I have made while working on the TR. My first day was spent with a couple digging holes for telegraph poles between Rhydyronen and Cynfal. I remember they were aghast that I did not know who Herbert Jones was, as he swept by on the afternoon train – they seemed to be in awe of him. A few years later, in the autumn of 1975, I fired to Herbert on trains terminating at Dolgoch and running forward to Quarry Siding to run round while Abergynolwyn was being prepared for the Nant Gwernol Extension. On another early visit, track work was under way at Pendre loop, and I was directed to sort scrap spikes from reusables. At that time tea breaks were taken in the old mess room – the remnants of the former cottage – when little boys were seen but not heard. The company included Don Southgate, John Bate, Ian Howitt and Richard Hope.

When I reached the age of 14 I started cleaning engines and had my first 'third man' trip on No 3 with Colin Roobottom and Dai Jones. As now, cleaners had to open the crossing gates, chop firewood, clear out the ashpit and so on. However, coal was still delivered by rail and I got roped into emptying the 13-ton wagons – shovelling out through the small door and onto the conveyor. I also remember the 'tide mark' on the landlady's bath that evening!

My first rostered firing turn was in September 1974, firing No 4 to Colin Roobottom on a rather wild and windy Saturday. Mark Winstanley was the guard and Carol Jones his assistant. I think Colin and I were the only available volunteers in the Loco Department that day, so it was a case of needs must I suppose. I have now completed 499 rostered firing trips (we'll have to see if there is a celebration with the next trip!), and I have fired to 39 different drivers. The 39th was Charlie Daniel, who remarked, 'I didn't know you were a fireman.' Well, it's true, I do a lot less firing these days than I used to and I am more usually associated with the outdoor gang and 'Tracksiders', but I was able to show him that I knew what I was doing!

In the mid-1970s the Pendre Blockman was the Loco Department's responsibility. I remember Tony Leaver and Bill Nicholls performing this duty when there was a lever frame at each end of the loop and the token and staff instruments were on the shelf in the loco shed. By the time I did some blocking myself Pendre had its new blockpost.

I left school in 1976 and that opened the way to join weekend working parties and the outdoor gang (and the informal London Area

Fireman Ian Evans looks out as *Dolgoch* comes up the loop at Abergynolwyn on 31 July 2007. *D. J. Mitchell*

meetings that organised lift-sharing). I therefore missed being a 'gwern', but did get involved in the subsequent development of the forest walks (when lunch was taken at the Railway Inn!). I've not kept a record of how many days I've done in the outdoor gang or all of the jobs done, but the list includes the night-time relaying below Abergynolwyn (especially memorable when Steve put his mattock through the temporary lighting circuit, plunging us all into darkness!); bringing the 10RB down from the Extension to regrade Wharf cutting (for the first time!) and getting it past the platforms; the tipping of ash, first on the sliding siding at Ty Mawr and later at Fach Goch (where Hugh Jones forgot to let go of the wagon!); working the old hedge-cutter with loco No 8 and having to pick the arisings out of the field, lest the sheep should get tangled up; and digging out the ballast at Plas Coch – except it wasn't really ballast, as the stabling of locos outside Hugh Jones's gate had left a compacted mix of oil and ash. There were also various relaying jobs during Outdoor Weeks, and works in connection with the Wharf redevelopment. I particularly enjoyed working with our wonderful YMG gang to reinstate the Wharf edge turntable.

I have enjoyed a number of holidays and outings with friends made on the TR, narrowboating and trips to the Isle of Man in particular. A day trip from Tywyn to Castletown, for a pub lunch, using the Llandudno to Douglas ferry was particularly memorable. In the mid-1980s I was a member of Council for six years, and the various sub-committees. I was on the London Area Committee for several years and helped with the sales stand at various model railway exhibitions, at one stage being the proud owner

An early working party just above Quarry Siding around milepost 5¾. *TR Collection*

of a grade card to operate Bob Hailes's 'Talyllyn Country' layout. I have given publicity talks, and more recently have become Trustee of the Narrow Gauge Railway Museum.

In about 1986 the *Tracksider* newsletter was started by Christopher Awdry for TRPS members aged 5 to 15 inclusive. Subsequently, several members expressed concern about the recruitment and retention of young volunteers. Winston McCanna initiated a discussion at TRPS Council in the autumn of 1996. He had done his homework, so when Council said 'Yes, but who?' he was able to nominate me! As a result I was appointed Project Leader for a new initiative to involve under-14s. The following May the first working party for families with younger members took place. The group chose to take the name 'Tracksiders', after the newsletter. We meet on the TR for Spring Bank Holiday week and in October half-term. Other visits are arranged as appropriate. We have also held training 'experience' events in Tywyn and at the Downs School in Colwall and North Ings Museum. The key thing, so far as I am concerned, is that Talyllyn 'Tracksiders' is arranged to provide opportunities, within a structured framework, for family participation. Attendance at the safety briefing before starting work each day

Encouraging youthful volunteering has always been an aim of the TR. These young volunteers are at work on the Extension in the 1970s. *TR Collection*

is mandatory. Families are then free to participate in a way that suits their own circumstances. We aim to run at least two jobs fairly close together, so that families can change jobs during the day. This provides variety and copes with the shorter attention spans of some participants. Of course 'Tracksiders' are responsible for under-14s, who are not allowed to work on the trains, although we do not set any specific age limits. Under-14s can only take part if they are accompanied by a parent, grandparent or guardian. This arrangement also provides a pool of supervisors, although we do not necessarily insist that children work with their own parents! The families are a wonderful bunch and that is a major factor in the 14 years of successful Tracksiding. By the end of 2010 Junior Members had contributed more than 2,500 'Tracksider days'. Another pleasing factor has been the number of former 'Tracksiders' now actively involved in TRPS volunteering, including my own daughter Clare.

'Tracksiders' work on projects such as painting, fencing, clearing undergrowth, restoring slate fencing, building footpaths and relaying sidings. We have done work at stations, on the lineside and in the Narrow Gauge Railway Museum, and support the May 'Duncan Days' with a model railway exhibition. We enjoy maintaining the Abergynolwyn play area and are gradually developing a sculpture and nature trail. However, we are not involved in the operating of trains, and Pendre workshops and sheds are effectively 'out of bounds' to 'Tracksiders'. The aim of course is to do something useful for our railway, to do so safely, perhaps learning new skills, to have fun and, importantly, to make new friends. That is the essence of the TR and what keeps bringing me back. We often get frustrated that Tywyn is so far from anywhere. However, the flipside is that those who come stay over. The other major part of the 'Tracksider' success is the social activities that happen in the evenings – picnics at Bearded Lake or Castell-y-bere, rounders on the beach, barbecues and the annual putting competition.

Tony Randall

In the summer of 1968 the Randall family had a holiday at a B&B on a farm north of Harlech. During the week my father and I visited all the narrow gauge railways that made up the 'Great Little Trains of Wales', which at that time was only the Ffestiniog Railway, the Snowdon Mountain Railway, the Fairbourne Railway, the Welshpool & Llanfair Light Railway, the Vale of Rheidol Railway and, of course, the Talyllyn Railway. The reason for the choice of our summer holiday in 1968 became clearer the following year, when my father and I had a week-long holiday during August in Towyn when he volunteered for the first time as a cleaner on the TR. Although only 13, I was also to help, my contribution being to work in the Wharf shop under the guidance of Eric Gibbons and Tris England. The following year I started as a trainee guard – my first three days were on the trains with 'The Green Man', aka John Cox, after which there was a mixture of station and train duties. August 1971 saw more of the same, and at the end of the fortnight I was

Tony Randall.

Volunteers' stories

Tony persuaded two of his workmates to volunteer on the TR, and one of them, Eric Nicholass, is seen here on the occasion of the 25th anniversary of him becoming a Guard. The train carries a special headboard ('Von Eric's Express'). The TR is like a family and celebrates major events in the volunteers' lives on the railway. *TR Collection*

handed my Assistant Guard grade card by David Woodhouse.

In 1972 I travelled to Tywyn alone for the first time during the school holidays, and the following year enjoyed my 'gap fortnight' between leaving school and starting work in mid-July. Trips to the railway could then become more frequent – a perk of my job with London Transport was to pay only one-quarter fare on British Rail trains – and my holiday entitlement was quite generous too.

After checking in at the B&B at which I would be staying, the next thing I normally did was to visit Wharf station and in particular the Guards' Room to see what duties I had been rostered for the week and with whom I would be working.

Like many other volunteers, I wanted to get promoted to Guard before thinking about other roles. That promotion came in 1975 when a volunteer succumbed to illness and I was asked what I intended to do on my day off that week – would I be able to guard on that day instead? Would anybody turn that chance down? Once I had consolidated my experience as a Guard I turned my attention to becoming a Blockman, in which role I was approved to work unsupervised in 1979.

At most workplaces a frequent topic of conversation is holidays – London Transport was no exception, and through talking about what I did on holiday in Wales on different occasions during the late 1970s I persuaded three colleagues who had become good friends to give the Talyllyn a try – two of them, Lawrie Bowles and Eric Nicholass, remain regular volunteers more than 30 years on. I also introduced two girlfriends to volunteering, and both qualified as Assistant Guards; the first, Elaine (also known as 'Nurse Gladys', because of her profession rather than any likeness to the original in Ronnie Barker's *Open All Hours*), stopped volunteering after a couple of years when we went our separate ways, and the second, Amanda, now Mrs Randall, also passed out as a Blockman, but did not really enjoy operating duties. Instead she found her niche where she could contribute much more to the railway through her IT skills and talents as the IT coordinator.

Increasing earnings with promotion at work and few financial commitments (still living at home!) meant that I used nearly all my holiday entitlement in the 1980s with visits to Tywyn, often at times when the railway was run with the minimum number of volunteers, so my range of experience widened considerably, particularly in the Wharf roles – Booking Clerk, Platform Inspector, then Controller. I thoroughly enjoyed working in the Wharf booking office, and take particular pride in balancing the cash against ticket sales at the end of the day in the large proof books. Wharf's booking office almost became my second home – when the TR opened an InterCity ticket agency in the early 1990s I found it most enjoyable to add this job to my portfolio. It was a requirement of the agreement that any ticket agency had a minimum number of staff who passed the Quality of Service examination, so I undertook this, and for some years some of my visits to Tywyn were fixed by the need to maintain

The Wharf booking office is on the extreme left. The other buildings were swept away and replaced by the present station building and Narrow Gauge Railway Museum, which was officially opened in July 2006. The TR might be a 'preserved railway' but it has moved with the times as far as passenger facilities are concerned. *TR Collection*

cover for the agency when Phil Care, the railway's Chief Clerk, who usually provided the agency service, was away.

My time working for the Talyllyn Railway has not been confined to the Traffic Department. I try to be in Tywyn for the Autumn Outdoor Week after daily train services finish each year, and take an active role with the London Area Group committee – as Treasurer for 20 years, and for a similar period as a Talyllyn Railway representative on the tripartite organising committee of 'Steampipes', an annual fund-raising film show that also supports the Ffestiniog and Welshpool & Llanfair railways. Another role I have undertaken occasionally is car park attendant at Wharf on days such as Easter Monday, when car-parking space in Tywyn is at a premium and many users of the car park are not intending to travel on the railway, so being on duty to take their car park fee means that the railway still gets its dues.

The Talyllyn does not have a uniform, in the strictest sense of the word, merely guidelines on what to wear. One day I saw an advertisement in a Sunday newspaper supplement for clothing that could be customised with any design of logo, so I wrote for details. The minimum initial order had to be 24 items, so I gambled on being able to sell 24 pullovers embroidered with the TRPS crest to other volunteers, and placed and paid for an order of what I thought would be the most likely sizes to sell. The completed pullovers were delivered to me shortly before a training seminar was to be held at Birmingham International station, so I packed them up and took them with me. Most were sold at the seminar, the more popular sizes sold out, and I took orders for more – the repeat orders with the manufacturer only needed to be for a minimum of six garments. Once the jumpers were seen in Tywyn many enquiries and orders followed, and for a number of years a regular advertisement in *Talyllyn News* enabled the London Area Group to benefit from the proceeds, albeit not the sort of profit margin a commercial venture would expect, as this was primarily

Volunteers' stories

intended as a service to both the railway and other volunteers. Eventually the market for these items slowed to a trickle, so I handed over the administration to a resident of Tywyn who was more accessible and able to handle any enquiries at the time.

In more than 40 years of staying in Tywyn I cannot claim the same loyalty to accommodation as some volunteers (but I've only moved on to another when I have not been able to book in at the last place where I stayed). For the first visit in 1969 my father and I stayed at 'Monfa' near the beach in Pier Road, the next couple of years saw me staying at 'Glantywodwyn', similarly close to the beach in Warwick Place. When I could not get in to 'Glantywodwyn', the Tywyn landlady network referred me Mrs Blowers at 'Llys Myfyr' (which is now the Welsh Property Shop). Mrs Blowers's illness forced another move, this time to 'The Romarian' (run at the time by Tony Read, and only open between Easter and the end of September). About this time I was joining outdoor winter working parties five or six times each winter, and as 'The Romarian' was not open I stayed at the Corbett Arms Hotel. I also stayed there over Christmas one year when it was unusually busy. When checking out, the new receptionist did not recognise me as a guest who (at that time) stayed there relatively frequently and gave me a copy of the hotel's advertising leaflet, presumably in an effort to get me to book another visit – it had the opposite effect, as the leaflet told me about the hotel's 37 comfortable rooms, and I had just checked out of Room 38!

Amanda and I married in 1989, and visits to Tywyn together were likely to remain frequent, so we looked around for a suitable pied-à-terre in Tywyn – we eventually bought a third-floor apartment at Trem Enlli, on the seafront, and probably one of the furthest places in Tywyn from Pendre, where most TR operating duties start and finish! It was a two-bedroom apartment, so we were able to have friends and family to stay with us – increasing volunteer effort into the bargain – and this also brought more new volunteers as Amanda's parents joined us, and on several occasions staffed the sales trolley at Dolgoch Falls station as their volunteering effort. Our apartment served us well, but the stairs up to the third floor were becoming a deterrent to both ourselves when encumbered with luggage and provisions when arriving late on a Friday night, and more generally to Amanda's parents, so we sold it and looked for something nearer to ground level. When 'Hen Efail' came onto the market it was exactly what we wanted, so we were delighted when it became ours in August 2002. The benefits were immediate – from one of the furthest places from Pendre to the closest!

Amanda Randall – and cat!

Amanda Randall

Tony, my husband, has been a volunteer on the Talyllyn since the age of 13. When I first met him I heard stories of the Talyllyn and came to believe that it was a 'boys and their toys' thing, something that I would not in a million years ever be interested in. How wrong I was, and little did I know what I was letting myself in for when I agreed to join him for a week in Tywyn.

My first volunteering visit was a week back in 1988. Tony and I were staying at 'The Romarian' bed and breakfast, it was July and tipping down with rain. I remember it well, thinking that it could only get better! That week was spent volunteering in the shop when Liz Green was the shop manager. It was a very enjoyable time and a great introduction to the many volunteers and the start of friendships that are still strong to this day. However, I decided that this was really not my sort of thing.

In the following year I was reluctantly persuaded once again to

Driver Alex Eyres looks out of the fireman's side of No 1 *Talyllyn* at Brynglas station on 3 March 2008. The blockpost can be seen at the end of the platform. *D. J. Mitchell*

join my now husband (Tony and I married in 1989) on a holiday in Tywyn working on the TR. In an effort to find something that I would really enjoy I was persuaded to try guarding. I was rostered as trainee with John Cox for my first day, followed by a day with Colin Bowles. I did enjoy those days but, to cut a long story short, I do not do early mornings (there are quite a few other members on the railway who will testify to that – there seems to be no pleasing me at times!).

Blocking was my preferred traffic duty. I could shut myself away in the Welsh countryside with a good book and only have to deal with the occasional interruption of a steam train passing by or a crossing. I have two abiding memories of my career as a Blockman, both of which happened at Brynglas. The first was when I was dealing with a crossing; I went out of the blockpost to collect the token from the up train, and when I returned I found the farm cat tucking in to my tuna fish sandwich! Following that I took pity on the cat, and whenever I was rostered there afterwards I always made sure I had a supply of cat biscuits to keep her away from my lunch. The second memory is of all-night steam in 1991. Tony and I were covering the night turn at Brynglas blockpost. Just after sunrise the farmer decided it was time to move his sheep across the line, and it seemed that every sheep that walked over the crossing took one look at us and started to bleat very loudly. They all seemed to be sticking their tongues out at us and the noise was incredible! I am sure they were just surprised to see us there at that time of the day.

Coming from a banking and IT background, the post of Wharf booking clerk appealed to me as a job where I could add some value. When I first started as a booking clerk the daily balancing was a manual task using huge bound ledgers and a lot of pencil work. The breakthrough into IT on the TR was the installation of TITAN, a system written by Brian Bushell primarily for the use of the Ffestiniog Railway but tweaked for the TR. It had some interesting report headings such as passenger loadings for Porthmadog with TR figures. It became apparent that this was not serving our purposes in the best way and I was asked by David Woodhouse, the General Manager at the time, if I could produce a new Traffic Office booking system that was more suited to the TR's operations. It was a great honour to be asked to do this, after such a short acquaintance with the railway, and I engaged in the task with enthusiasm. It was also the start of a seemingly ever-increasing involvement with the Talyllyn.

Railways make great use of acronyms to describe almost anything, so it was important to have a snappy and appropriate name for the new system (not as easy as it sounds!). It took a surprising amount of time to come up with something that the majority of volunteers liked. After much debate the name TRACS (Talyllyn Railway Accounting for Cash System) was agreed. This was followed by a considerable amount of time building the new application (and lots of testing to ensure that it was error-free) and a few late nights in the booking office transferring data

Volunteers' stories

from the old system. TRACS Version 1 went into operation in June 1993 and remained more or less the same for 15 years, which is an achievement of which I am immensely proud.

However, times move on and IT systems have to keep up. A change in the Society Treasurer and Company Accountant in 2005 – it is a quirk of the TR that you get elected to a Society post and by default fulfil a similar role for the railway company – led to the new person seeing that TRACS could be put to even better use in providing control, reports and analysis of revenue and passenger travel trends. Changing TRACS to meet these requirements has proved to be extremely interesting and has provided me with some tough challenges. As with anything these days, TRACS often needs updating to accommodate new services that the railway offers, or somebody may come up with an idea to improve something or to add something that is not already catered for. There are also the smaller applications that I have produced that need attention from time to time (Ticket Stocks and Guards Journal recording). I am certainly kept occupied!

I now hold the honorary position of IT Coordinator, appointed by Council. One of the more recent challenges has been to provide the railway with a stable IT infrastructure that does not require a permanent presence in Tywyn to maintain and look after it, so I recommended that the TR moved to a remote system, which means that I can now manage the railway's systems from Kent and the Company Accountant can access the information from Essex. The beauty of this is that it minimises the equipment in Tywyn that needs to be maintained thanks to the internet connection and our remote services provider.

Although I can access most things remotely to fulfil my role as IT Coordinator, it can never replace the sheer enjoyment I get from visiting Tywyn. Tony and I try to make sure there is never a period of more than four weeks between visits; it is often more frequently that we make the 280-mile journey from Rochester to Tywyn to our house just opposite Pendre station. One of the things that I love about it is that it is almost impossible to go out into the front garden without having a conversation with somebody. A quick 30-minute job to clean the windows has in the past turned in to a half-day job purely because there is always somebody to say 'hello' to – something I would never want to change.

The most ironic thing about all of this is I am now probably even more involved in the railway than my husband is, something I would never have believed if I had been told back in 1988!

Lawrence Garvey

I first came across the Talyllyn Railway as the result of an article in the *Railway Roundabout* Annual for 1961. However, I did not visit the TR until some years later, in either 1966 or 1967, when I went on a Midland Red day trip from Birmingham, and travelled from Wharf to Dolgoch Falls on what I recall as being a very crowded train. My next visit was not until Easter 1970, having joined the TRPS earlier that year after having been given a membership form at Warley Model Railway Show the previous year.

My first visit was only for three days. I managed to arrive late on the first day, then spent time sat on Wharf station platform reading what seemed very incomprehensible Rule Books and Working Instructions. The next morning I recall arriving at Pendre and sweeping out stock in the dark of the South Carriage Shed before spending my first full day as a trainee guard. By the end of the day it seemed as if I had been on a ship; even when standing on firm ground I still felt as if I were swaying from side to side. The following morning I was not due to start work until the second train of the day, so went from Dolgoch to Abergynolwyn to look at the early work that was taking place there in preparation for the extension to Nant Gwernol, which was to be the start of a long involvement with the engineering side of the Talyllyn.

That early visit led to me returning in July, to Towyn, as it then was, on my own, travelling by train to stay at 'Monfa' on Pier Road. I spent an enjoyable week, including going with a number of other volunteers to visit the Festiniog Railway and walking the routes proposed for the Deviation Project. The final visit of that year was to be by special train for the AGM, travelling from Birmingham with a number of Midlands-based volunteers.

As was common in those days, I was not to visit the Talyllyn for a further 12 months, this time for a fortnight after finishing school for the summer holidays. The ballast dock was being dug by then and I acted as guard on a number of engineering trains up and down to Fach Goch. Another 12 months elapsed before I returned, this time to stay at No 5 Brynmair with Don and Doris Southgate. No 5 was home to many volunteers and the Talyllyn tended to be the main topic of conversation at breakfast, dinner and supper. In fact, this was to become my second home for a number of years, for once I had learned to drive my visits to Tywyn increased greatly, often giving lifts to other volunteers as there were no trains from Tywyn on Sundays. I was also splitting my time between working in the Traffic Department when needed and undertaking engineering work.

1976 saw the opening of the extension to Nant Gwernol and I was to spend ten long days at Tywyn over the Easter holiday week working to install signal cables and other signalling equipment at Abergynolwyn. It seemed but a very short period before returning to be present at the opening ceremony.

Life had also become a little more complex, as I had met Jane in Tywyn, and she was to become my wife in 1979. However, she lived in Southampton, so I was travelling a great deal. At our wedding there were a large number of TRPS members and the event had a distinctly railway feel to it.

We continued to live in Birmingham and I soon found myself involved in the Midland Area Group, as Working Party Organiser, together with spells as Secretary and Chairman. At this time we regularly gave lifts to three young members, all of whom are now drivers on the Talyllyn; two married girls from Tywyn and one now manages a miniature railway nearby. So it's entirely our fault.

We then found ourselves having somewhat less time to devote to the Talyllyn Railway as our family arrived, all at once in the shape of twins, Richard and Elizabeth. For a couple of years we were restricted to a single annual visit; however, in 1988 we acquired, as a family, thanks to my parents, a caravan in Tywyn, which enabled us to visit on a far more

Lawrence Garvey on blockpost duty. *R. J. Morland*

regular basis. At this time I also changed my employment, moving to work for British Rail Civil Engineer London Midland Region as a Charted Quantity Surveyor. I gained extra holidays and the ability to travel to Tywyn very cheaply as a result. Winters were still difficult times as our caravan was not available, so visits were restricted to those times we could borrow cottages, often over the New Year period when Jane would be involved with catering for New Year parties and selecting pictures for the calendar.

We continued to visit Tywyn over the next few years, working alternate days, unless we could persuade our parents to look after our children, until the start of 'Tracksiders', when we went out as a family to work on the railway. The first year of 'Tracksiders' could not have been better, with warm sunny working days followed by evening entertainment and barbecues. Many friendships were forged by both parents and children that have lasted to this day.

The fateful day then arrived when the Membership Secretary announced he wanted to retire, so after much discussion Jane and I put our names forward as a joint team. Council accepted our offer and we found ourselves travelling from Birmingham to Croydon to collect the computer and associated paperwork, as well as learning how it worked. This task was then to occupy our lives when we were not at work – there always seemed to be something to be done, and in 1999 we realised that the 'Millennium Bug' might strike, so we needed to commission a new computer and membership database. We made it by the skin of our teeth, thanks to a lot of assistance from the IT specialist in the Society.

We continued to come to Tywyn over the years using our caravan until 2003, when we were fortunate enough to find ourselves able to swap the caravan for a small cottage a few minutes walk from Pendre. This marked a change in our involvement, as we were now able to come to Tywyn whenever we wanted to, winter or summer, so we found our time there increasing. By now Richard and Elizabeth were volunteering in their own right and as keen as we were to be in Tywyn, although we did manage to get away on holiday occasionally. However, every spare weekend seemed to be spent in Tywyn, with less and less time spent in Birmingham.

It did not seem that we had had our cottage for long before we decided that we wanted to make a change in our lives. We had for many years considered running a bed and breakfast business, so made a decision to look for a suitable property in Tywyn. This took some time, but in January 2006 we found a suitable house, strangely enough three doors away from No 5 Brynmair where we had both spent many years in the 1970s; after much work we opened for business in March 2007. Jane had given up her teaching job in late 2006 to move to Tywyn, but I continued to work in Birmingham until October 2008, commuting backwards and forwards each week, before finding I could take very early retirement.

In 2009 we indicated to Council that we wanted to retire as Membership Secretaries in 2010, as running our own business meant we were not available at the peak of the renewal 'season', being away on our annual holiday. We handed over the work in June 2010, but we became even more involved with assisting the Talyllyn in Tywyn. I found myself appointed as Volunteer Coordinator to give prospective volunteers a person to contact and hopefully to encourage members to come and spend time working on the railway. I also found myself Project Managing a number of schemes on behalf of the company, which will hopefully improve the railway for both our passengers and future volunteers.

Our children have also become a part of the Talyllyn family. Our son Richard is now a Fireman, Guard and Blockman, having spent many summers in Tywyn, railway work has also become the norm for him, as he is a Signalling Technician for Network Rail. Elizabeth went to university, also spending her summers in Tywyn, mainly working for the café, of which she was appointed joint manager in 2009.

Over the years I have undertaken many roles for the TR, qualifying as a Guard, Blockman, Controller, Diesel Driver and Rail Incident Officer. I also spend time each week working with the outdoor gang, and am a regular volunteer during Outdoor Weeks. The Talyllyn has over the years become an integral part of our daily lives, even more so with our move to Tywyn. Jane is a member of Council and a Traffic Inspector, and our home is a regular calling point for volunteers of all ages.

I suspect that the Talyllyn will continue to be a major factor in our lives. We certainly do not intend to move away from Tywyn, where we now have many friends, and where we are a part of the local community.

Ken Timson

Ken Timson lighting up. *R. J. Morland*

have picked out a number of what I think of as the most noteworthy incidents to happen to me.

Most of the 477 firing trips I have undertaken have passed without major upset, just the usual interesting mixture of trying to give the driver the required steam pressure, keeping the water level well in sight, giving the correct signals and maintaining a good lookout – sometimes a struggle, but always a joy. I see from my records that I have fired to 44 drivers during my time on the TR. I count myself lucky to have been on the footplate with Herbert, Hugh, Dai and David Jones, all a pleasure to work with. Fifty-five

It was Easter 1971 when my son Trevor, then 12, and I first came as volunteers to Tywyn. We had just 'volunteered' and didn't know where we might be directed. We went first to Wharf and were shown the rosters in the Guards' Room, but couldn't see our names anywhere. We were told to go to Pendre, where we discovered our names on the cleaners' board. For me that was the start of a love affair with the railway. We did a fortnight a year for the next three years, with Trevor doing a month in the year he was 16, desperate to get his passed cleaner's ticket. That year, when we finished, Herbert Jones approached Trevor and said, 'I suppose you'll be wanting this then?' and held out his cleaner's ticket, which had been handed in for date-stamping. At the moment that Trevor reached for it Herbert turned his hand to reveal a beautiful new Passed Cleaner ticket! Success! It was a double success as I had just been given my Fireman's card. In what follows I

of my trips were with Maurice Wilson, who was very supportive in my early years, and let me get on with it as I grew in experience – something that some drivers do not do very often. More than 40 were with John Scott, which are always intellectually stimulating – more than 20 with Bill Faulkner, Phil Guest, Roy Smith and John Robinson. Bill tended to be rather taciturn on the footplate; I suspected I was rostered to him because, being older, I didn't chatter too much! However, I remember one trip where we had taken Ian Evans as third man on the first trip, and approaching Pendre I turned and knocked my shovel off the footplate! Ian nipped out onto the platform and went back to retrieve it. We carried on to Wharf, and, it seemed, had only just arrived when Ian came running up with the missing shovel. Bill was so pleased with his effort that he gave him a second third man trip – something that very rarely happened!

I have my favourites, those with whom you can have a good natter and a laugh, like Jonathan Mann and Mike Green, and there are others who are a bit of a pain – but no names, no pack drill! As a fireman one has to adjust to suit your driver, most of whom are a pleasure to be with. On 12 July 1977 I was with Bill Faulkner on No 3. There had been trouble with a steam joint in the smokebox, which had had to be welded up, but it had gone again by the time we reached Wharf with the stock. It proved to be an exciting trip, as half the steam being produced was escaping. Bill had the regulator right across, the fire was white hot, steam everywhere, and we used the whole bunker of coal on one trip. The engine did all three trips, No 1 banking us to Pendre on the second and third, and Duncan Ritchie firing on the third. When it got back, No 3 was withdrawn, a new steam pipe was fabricated and the whole was put back together in very quick time – three days if I remember correctly.

One day in 1979 I was just coaling up when Colin Roobottom came up with the news that No 8 had failed up the line. Although Colin was the rostered driver, Bill jumped on and we shot up the line on a rescue mission. The first up train was about due. Unfortunately my log doesn't go into any detail about what happened when we reached No 8, only that the rest of the day went well! In 1980 I took part in another rescue mission, also with Bill driving. I was on No 4, on the stock, with about 60 on the clock when the news came that No 1 had failed at Dolgoch. It was decided that we should pilot the 10.25, so we went down to Wharf and coupled onto No 3 (John Scott driving, Terry Gurd firing). Bill obviously thought that we should be doing most of the work – my pressure had come up to about 100 by that point and Bill had the regulator right over. Meanwhile No 3 was blowing off. We continued up the line until Dolgoch Viaduct, when a guard waving a red flag appeared in the near distance and simultaneously we went over two detonators. The noise was so loud I thought the wheels had been blown off! We uncoupled and ran into Dolgoch platform. The passengers of the earlier train were waiting on the platform to join the 10.25. We propelled the complete train up to Quarry, then the 10.25 went on up the line. When clear, we proceeded to take the empty stock and No 1 back to Tywyn. Bill was concerned that we shouldn't cause too much disruption of the timetable and we rattled back, dropping off No 1 at Pendre; its motion was damaged and had to be stripped down and straightened.

My next 'incident' was seven years later. On 20 August I had an evening train with John McDougall driving. On the way back we ran over a sheep – I have to admit that we hardly felt a thing! In our defence it was a very dark evening and the engine lamp doesn't give much illumination. Iolo Davies buried it the following morning.

In 1988 John Scott ran a coal economy week. The coal was from Oakdale. On Friday 12 August I was with John on No 4 and we brought the consumption down by 3 kilos to 142kg. On 5 August 1991 I was with John Robinson on No 2 and was taking the empty stock to Pendre after a good day, although very wet. As I approached the stop board, I applied the steam brake and the handle came off in my hand! A jet of steam hit the back plate with a great roar. John managed to bundle Tim (the third man) out of the fireman's side, applied the hand brake, then nipped out to close the shut-off valve. No one was hurt, but it was a few seconds of excitement that we could have done without. On 8 August, with Dave Scotson driving, John Timpson (of the BBC) rode up in the Corris coach collecting material for a book (*Little Trains of Britain*, published by Harper-Collins). We often have to contend with sheep on the line, but on that day we met a bullock, which turned and ambled towards us. It took a lot of arm waving and shouting to get it moving, until, to our surprise, it jumped the fence. I had a chat with my namesake back at Wharf, and later, reading the book, found that I had a 'mention'.

The following day was my first trip on No 7. I believe it was also Maurice Wilson's first trip. We started off in fine style, so imagine my horror when, opening the firebox door as we approached Brynglas, I could see the firebars! Having collected the token we went into the platform, where we stayed a couple of minutes more while the repaired fire recovered. It appears that the blastpipe was too small and gave excessive draw when the regulator was opened up. It was enlarged a bit and the problem disappeared. From Dolgoch we had a correspondent from a railway weekly with us so I'm glad to say that everything went well.

On 6 August 1997, during 'Victorian Week', I was on No 3 with John Scott on 'The Royal Train', that is taking 'Queen Victoria' up to

Abergynolwyn. Horror of horrors – I had to stop for a blow-up on Doldeheuwydd Bank! Too thin a fire at the front was compounded by enormous lumps of coal, which allowed cold air between – bang went my MBE!

On my first trip with Don Newing (3 August 1999) we had a sad duty to perform – to cremate the Brynglas cat, which had been found dead under the blockpost. On the same day I had a 'magic' evening train with Gareth Jones.

In Golden Jubilee Week 2001 there were some very complicated working timetables run. On the Tuesday of that week I was on No 6, and we had two whole trips as the train engine, three turns piloting in various places, light engine from Abergynolwyn to Quarry Siding, and banking the 15.20 to Pendre.

For many years the TR and the townspeople of Tywyn organised a 'Victorian Week' in August. Here 'Queen Victoria' (aka Sally Roberts) and Richie Owen get the 'red carpet' treatment from Roger Whitehouse as they board the Corris coach. In the background the fireman is the late Tony Bennett, who was in the Marines, then a police officer in West Yorkshire. *TR Collection*

Sara Eade

My first encounter with the Talyllyn Railway was in the summer of 1971 when I and my family had our last family holiday before my brother, Richard, went to university in London and I went back to Trinity College, Carmarthen, to finish my third year in Teaching and Youth & Community Studies. We came for a week to look at the 'Great Little Trains of Wales' and travelled on the TR every day, sometimes at the beginning of the day before going off to visit one of the other railways, and sometimes at the end of the day, when we would get Dad to drop us off at Abergynolwyn for the last down train, then he and Mum would go back to the bungalow at Pall Mall Farm to cook tea. We were fascinated by the railway, the engines, the carriages and the 'frothy coffee' at Abergynolwyn. We were hooked, and my brother and I joined the Society in September 1971.

The following summer we booked in for our first fortnight as volunteers and stayed at Reg Palk's caravan at Tynllwynhen. Reg worked with my Dad at Swindon Borough Council and for many years was involved with the Museum. We arrived at Pendre on our first working day knowing nothing and no one, and were met by John Smallwood, who quickly made us feel at home and put us to work. In those days we learned on the job and were privileged to learn from experienced 'old hands' – it was some years

Volunteers' stories

later that we found some of these had been new volunteers themselves only the year before.

During that first fortnight we had experience as trainee guards, station assistants, control assistants, carriage cleaners and 'bodgers'. One of the first things we learned was Rule No 1 – DO NOT BE PARTED FROM YOUR LUNCH. In those days it meant making sure you took your food with you, as it could be a long time before you had chance to eat it if you had left it behind.

The days were long, the trains full and the sun always seemed to be shining. It was great and the experience was added to by the evening entertainment – walking over Barmouth Bridge for a drink, 'Grutting on the Peen', cricket on the playing-field and dropping into the Corbett Arms Hotel just before last orders. Occasionally we would walk down to the seafront for 'chicken in the basket' and a game of pool at the Ddraig Goch before dipping our toes in the sea in the moonlight!

It was also during this fortnight that I had my first encounter with the Corris Railway, as Richard Greenhough was also a volunteer. He spoke so passionately about what they were doing that I joined their Society and was given member number 182 – who would have guessed that almost 40 years later I would also be volunteering there as well!

I am reliably informed by Mike Green that I made an impression on those working in the workshop, for when asked if I had the time, I apparently replied 'if you have the inclination'. There was no sending me for 'a long wait', 'a sky hook' or 'a left-handed screwdriver'!

I had a bit of a break from volunteering on the TR until Christmas 1974 when my brother bought me a weekend at Mrs Jones's (No 11 Cambrian Terrace) as a present, and that was enough to get me hooked again. By now I had a car and an income so could come to Tywyn as often as work would allow.

I trained as a Guard, getting my ticket in 1980, and since then have been involved with the Railway Letter Service – as Postmaster for 20 years and also on the Committee as now. The Railway Letter Service has made a major contribution to the railway over the years, and even though First Day Covers and railway letter stamps are not as popular as they once were, the TR still provides the service it started in 1957.

I have worked on the track, helped with

The TR has operated a Railway Letter Service since 1957. In 2003 Royal Mail approached the Talyllyn Railway to take photographs for a set of six stamps. A whole day was spent with a vintage train taking photographs at various locations on the line, and from these Royal Mail chose one of No 2 *Dolgoch* emerging from Rhydyronen bridge. As an example of the lengths to which photographers will go to get the effect they want, the bridge was sprayed with a hosepipe for about 20 minutes before the desired effect was achieved and the photographs taken! The collection of stamps was called 'Classic Locomotives' and a special train was run on 13 January 2004 to publicise the stamps. This envelope was signed by the train crew and is marked 'To be posted on arrival at Tywyn Wharf Station'.

producing one of the guidebooks, helped in the shop under Liz Green, Maria Wagland and Teresa Cox, and for several years worked with Crugwen at Abergynolwyn on Sundays making sandwiches, wrapping cakes and selling teas, coffees and hot chocolate.

I have spent many hours 'bodging' in the

paint shop, made antimacassars, re-covered seats, painted thin lines on TR coaches, filled, rubbed down, painted, undercoated and varnished, weeded the garden at Rhydyronen, collected rubbish, cleaned toilets and the mess room at Pendre – and then there was 'Victorian Week'. I was there at the beginning when the craft fairs were just a few of us at Abergynolwyn. I made quiches and salads and trifles when the New Year's Eve 'do' was in the Carriage Shed, I drove one of the diesels under instruction and put on craft exhibitions as part of the Tom Rolt Rally. When the extension was opened, I went round with a microphone and tape recorder, recording the noise of the event for a video – I wonder whatever happened to that?

I stood for Council once but was pipped at the post by Ed Lund; those were the days when it was really hard for female volunteers to get onto Council, but I did not let that put me off and continued to visit as often as I could.

The TR is very much like a large family and I have made some long-lasting friendships. Some of the people I got to know right at the beginning now have children and grandchildren and I am friends now with three generations in some cases.

And there are always the characters! I remember meeting John Slater in London once and being taken to see my first live Gilbert and Sullivan operetta. I used to clean for him at Caxton Cottage in exchange for a bottle of wine. Then there was the time I surprised him by covering his settee and chairs with bright sunny covers, taking away the dowdy look of the dark brown leather, which he hated. He was always very appreciative of anything done for him that allowed him a little more time at Pendre! Then there was the time that Mike Green and I went to Kew Pumping Station together, and who should we bump into but John – we then featured in that week's 'Slateoid'.

Phil Glazebrook, who came up from Watford, occasionally picked me up at Rugby, then the race was on to get to the Cross Foxes before 10.30 as we knew we could not get to Tywyn before last orders.

I also recall the annual canal trips with John Smallwood, Malcolm Phillips, John Burton, Andrew Powell, Martin Flach, Mark Winstanley, Peter Leppard, Ed Lund, Viv Thorpe, David Lawrence, David Lowe and others whose names I have forgotten. I remember one particular trip as we had a full boat for most of the week and the cost per person, including all the food, worked out to be £69 69p! Many's the night we have sat in a pub somewhere and put the railway to rights!

There were lots of fun times, there was always laughter, especially at tea break time. There was the Valentine's card sent to a member of the permanent staff via a friend of mine in Cheltenham, there was the day when John Bate came into work with orange hair, and the

Sara used to clean the late John Slater's cottage. A volunteer for many years, John is seen here still hard at work in Pendre Works on 8 September 1991. *R. J. Morland*

Volunteers' stories

day he cut my hair at a tea break with tin snips after a dare. There were the late nights getting a carriage repaint finished, the building of the West Carriage Shed, shampooing the carpet in the café at Wharf and hoping it would dry before morning, painting Wharf shop and sitting round eating fish and chips together after we had finished… Ah, they were the best of times.

When my parents were persuaded to move to Tywyn from Swindon, they got involved too and during the summer Dad could be found at Abergynolwyn selling his notelets, calendars and paintings, donating part of the proceeds to the TR. Mum used to make cakes, and when loco No 4 *Edward Thomas* had a 70th birthday, Mum made a cake, I iced it and everyone who attended the birthday party at Abergynolwyn enjoyed it, including the visitors from Corris.

When you get involved with the TR you can't avoid the connection with the slate quarry at Bryn Eglwys, and following a trip up to the quarry with Mike Green in his Land Rover I became fascinated with slate generally and now spend time researching the slate quarries in the area and have written two books.

Today I still do some work with the Railway Letter Service, and I'd like to think that all the training and experience on the TR was in preparation for helping out at the Corris – thank you Talyllyn for injecting the steam into my veins, for starting my interest in the narrow gauge, for the book and postcard collections, and for all the many friends I have made. Here's to the next 60 years!

Marshall Vine

I joined the Talyllyn Loco Department almost by accident! Having started to build a model of No 6 *Douglas*, I wrote asking if I could photograph and measure it. The railway was most helpful, but while I was crawling all over it Herbert Jones, then Loco Superintendent, crept up behind me and said, 'What do you want to make a model of it for when you could come here and play with the big one?' That hadn't actually occurred to me, but it was the start of many happy years commuting to Tywyn, and the model never did get finished. During this time I kept a daily diary. What it did show was that life on the TR footplate was rarely dull!

Reading the diary many years later it became obvious that animals played a significant part in the railway's operation. The odd sheep was hardly worth recording, but occasionally things became a bit more fraught! On 26 August 1973, for instance, when crews did three trips to Abergynolwyn, I noted that on the first trip there were sheep on the line at Dolgoch, on the second trip a cow at Fach Goch, and to complete the set on our third trip there was a pig on the line at Hendy.

Hendy was to figure much more prominently a couple of years later, when the events of Saturday 28 August 1976 could almost make a book on their own! The day started badly when No 8 failed, trapping the stock for the first train, but this was eventually sorted out. I was on No 3, on the second train, the empty stock for which arrived down at Wharf more or less on time. But we were delayed by a fire at Brynglas, which blocked the line, making us 20 minutes late off Wharf, not helped by late passengers for an already full train. There were other delays for various reasons all day, with the result that an already quick turn-round at Wharf for our last trip was reduced to only 3 minutes!

On the down run the Hendy sheep again took a hand, causing more delay with 12 of them on the line. These sheep must have told all their friends because when the last train came down after us there were about 20-30 of them, while it was reported the next day that the evening train was also delayed at Hendy, probably by the same sheep. A passenger apparently reckoned he counted 37 before he dozed off!

Then one day in 1978, on No 4, we came across six cows ambling down the track near Fach Goch. This of course was long before

Marshall Vine aboard *Sir Haydn*. *Marshall Vine collection*

continuous brakes, and we were travelling quite fast, but by whistling up for the van brakes to be applied we stopped in time. It apparently caused some consternation in the van, though!

I recorded several other incidents over the years, including one while I was duty shedman, when a number of us from Pendre spent the whole afternoon, mostly in pouring rain, chasing various sheep between Pendre and Hendy, getting them back through the fence and trying to repair the holes through which they had escaped. On another occasion we were preceded into Nant Gwernol by the six sheep we had picked up on the Extension.

Things that fall off engines! The Talyllyn Railway film of the early days, *Railway with a Heart of Gold*, shows at one point a young fireman picking up something that had supposedly fallen off the engine. Thankfully years of care and careful maintenance have made this far less likely, but my diary entries do record several times when it happened.

The first of these items was my watch, which had an expanding strap. The loco was No 2, and nearing Hendy bridge on an up train I managed to get the watch strap caught on the injector water valve, breaking the strap and firing the watch off the loco! I was able to catch a later train to Hendy Halt and luckily found it.

However, another item to go overboard a year or so later needed more immediate attention. It was the firing shovel. No 1 had just had a comprehensive rebuild and one of the alterations changed the shape of the coal bunker. Suddenly the little corner where you could safely leave your shovel wasn't there any more! It was all right if you remembered, but a moment's forgetfulness and before you could do anything about it the shovel had gone! It's very embarrassing going to pick it up after an unscheduled stop in the middle of nowhere – even worse, I should imagine, if you didn't miss it until needed later, as I was told had once happened.

By far the worst thing to lose is the single-line token, which gives your train the authority to proceed. I only ever did this once, and I claim mitigating circumstances. On No 4 one day, when the line ended at Abergynolwyn, the Quarry to Abergynolwyn section was then on the staff and ticket system, not the usual key token. The 'staff' was a heavy metal bar with a 'ticket' at each end, and had a bayonet connector on each end so they could be separated. It travelled on the loco in a little box on the fireman's side of the cab. Unfortunately on No 4 the box was too near the cab roof for the whole assembly, so on receiving it the fireman had to split it, removing one of the 'tickets'. One of the bayonet fittings was as stiff as blazes, so a hard twist was needed to unlock it. To get a better purchase I used to hold it mainly by the two 'tickets' – one always unclipped before the other. Not on this occasion, though, as unknown to me someone had freed off the stiff end. Having received the complete staff I gave it its usual twist only to be left holding the two tickets with the staff seeming to hover unsupported in the middle! It couldn't land on the footplate of course, but disappeared over the side. Fortunately we were still accelerating away from the Quarry blockpost so I didn't have far to go back for it.

Probably the oddest thing to fall off an engine was a face! It was during No 3's first year as *Sir Handel*. The face was a large fibreglass moulding,

Volunteers' stories

No 4 *Edward Thomas* brings its train over Dolgoch Viaduct on its way to Nant Gwernol. The driver is the late Phil Guest, and hopefully the single-line token is still safely stowed in the cab! *TR Collection*

and one morning before going off shed it fell off the loco and went into the pit. The result was a crack across Sir Handel's forehead, and no time to repair it. I can't remember who thought of it, but a quick trip to the first aid box for a bandage and some sticky tape had a slightly wounded *Sir Handel* back in service and getting a great deal of sympathy from our young passengers. The loco ran for several days like this until the face could be repaired properly.

Some bits only nearly fall off, but still manage to cause a great deal of trouble. One such was a little screw on one of No 2's leading crankpin covers. Everything on Thursday 25 August was normal until just before Rhydyronen on our second trip when a rhythmic clonk was heard from somewhere on the fireman's side. Inspection in the station showed that a crankpin cover screw had worked loose, and was chewing up both itself and the back of the crosshead. By now it was too badly damaged to be just screwed back in, and could only get worse. Control was advised and it was decided to change engines with the down train at Brynglas so that No 2 could be worked gently back to Pendre. We therefore went slowly up to Brynglas, knocking all the time, and stopped at the lower stop board. Engines were changed and, by now horribly late, off we went, now with No 3. As she had been working a down train until only a few minutes previously, the fire was a bit thin, but we managed. Having arrived at Dolgoch we were told that as we were so late Control had arranged that we should pass the next down train at Quarry, which we did. We were greeted at Abergynolwyn by the blockman with, 'I'm surprised they gave you another engine after you broke the first one!'

Probably my most embarrassing day on the TR was when I had a bit fall off a wagon, although I must admit it did get a bit of help. I'd been asked to take No 8 down to Wharf and collect a wooden-framed wagon chassis for repair at Pendre. This wagon was well up the front siding at Wharf, well overgrown by weeds and brambles and obviously hadn't moved for a considerable time, but we oiled it and eventually got it coupled to No 8 in the far loop. We then waited for a clear path back up the line. At that time No 8's hydraulic gearbox was 'a bit iffy', to put it mildly. The position of the control lever in the cab didn't necessarily correspond with what the gearbox did. Finally getting a token and a 'right away', I eased the lever into what should have been a nice sedate forward motion. Nothing happened, so a bit more 'welly', then the loco took off with a hell of a jerk. Unfortunately our train didn't. There was a sort of creaking thump from behind, after which we could be seen towing the wagon headstock (the end beam where the coupling goes), and this bit only, along the rails. Of course all this took place right outside Wharf office and was difficult to hide, so out came 'Traffman', David Woodhouse, to politely ask if we intended to take it up the line. 'It', and the rest of the wagon, went back in the brambles for someone else to deal with!

These few reminiscences are by no means unusual. Many volunteers must have had similar experiences. Nor are they exhaustive. I could go on about the period when many loco fires went out during the long Abergynolwyn layover due to poor coal, or the time when the old carriage shed doors at Pendre, which for years had opened outwards, just once opened inwards, having been given a gentle push by two steam locos coupled together, the crews of which each thought the other would do the braking! Or what happens when you stop suddenly with the cabless No 9 when coupled in front of the 'Boflat' with a very large open-topped water tank on board…

I hope these reminiscences don't give the wrong impression. They took place over many weeks spread over even more years. Most of the time the Talyllyn jogs uneventfully along giving pleasure to both passenger and volunteer alike. But after many years one basic question, put to me many years ago now, still remains unanswered – are the volunteers there for the benefit of the passengers, or are the passengers there for the benefit of the volunteers?

Winston McCanna

I first encountered the Talyllyn in the flesh when our young family was holidaying in the area in the 1960s. It was only later that I realised it was the same railway that I had heard my father talk to Bill Trinder and Tom Rolt about in Bill's shop on a Saturday morning during the late 1940s. Unfortunately my parents had moved home miles away by the time 1950 came and I lost track of the Talyllyn.

My first TR activities were in the Wessex Area Group and very quickly I was asked to become first the Group's Publicity Officer and then its Chairman through the 1970s. My career as a TR engineman also started at this time. Professionally I was working for the Admiralty as a research engineer, and when I mentioned to my line manager on one occasion that I had been elected to the TRPS Council (this would have been in 1980) I soon received an approach from the Army Railway Organisation, who were seeking engineers who knew something about railways, to enquire if I would join them. Such an offer was too good to refuse and from then on my career took a quite different path,

Winston McCanna.

Volunteers' stories

and I eventually became the Organisation's Chief Engineer, so my TR activities had a direct and very profound effect upon my life.

On Council I filled a number of different roles through the 1980s, serving on the Marketing, Traffic & Operating, Finance & General Purposes, Museum and Engineering committees at times and being Chairman of the last two for lengthy periods. In 1987 came my election as Council's Vice Chairman, and this was followed three years later by being elected Chairman of Council. Additionally, and at the same time, I was appointed as a Director on the Board of the TR Company and Talyllyn Holdings. As a Board member I assumed responsibility to the Board for Health & Safety issues, and one of the measures I put in place was the annual Health & Safety Audit, which was carried out by an independent examiner. In this way the railway's affairs were raised to fully comply with legislation. Then the Railway Safety Critical Work regulations were published, and this meant first a review of what we did, then the introduction of new measures to ensure compliance. Some of these steps were not popular in some quarters, but now the sense of them is fully appreciated.

It was also during this period that a new Chief Executive was required and a small group, known as the men in grey suits, interviewed a number of us by invitation to sound us out regarding a replacement. I was about to retire from my position with the Army Rail Organisation, but still lived in Wiltshire and, until our permanent home was in Tywyn, taking on the role was not an option. In the event Maurice Wilson took on the challenge, initially as Company Chairman also, but when my home was established in Tywyn I became the Company Chairman to relieve Maurice and take some of the burden.

This arrangement carried on until 2000, when I decided that it was time to retire from Board and Council and I stood down. The nicest remark that was made to me at this time was by a member of staff who said that they admired someone who retired when they still had something to offer. Upon standing down I was then elected as a Vice President, an honour of which I am very proud.

In the mid-1980s I introduced my uncle, John McCanna, to the railway. He was a highly skilled cabinet-maker and pattern-maker and was about to retire. I persuaded him to undertake the task of building a new carriage for the TR and over the course of about eight summers that is what he did. The outcome is Van 7, the first carriage on the TR specifically designed for conveying wheelchair-bound passengers, and is probably as well constructed as any in our carriage fleet. It was introduced into service with a special event where the first passengers in the carriage were disabled ex-servicemen.

During all this time I continued with my great love on the Talyllyn, as a footplateman. Turns were becoming scarcer by now as more and more became qualified to fill them, but living locally I was in the right place when a short-term vacancy arose. I did many memorable turns, including

Fireman Winston McCanna on loco No 7 *Tom Rolt*. D. J. Mitchell

the very first on an Awdry 'Skarloey' engine on the TR in 1982. I also was asked to carry out a lot of blocking turns and was a controller for a number of years. My final loco turn was the Carol Train in 2006, and a bit of a fuss was made of me. I had asked for this turn for a number of years as it is still the only turn in the public timetable where both directions are guaranteed to be in the dark, and this makes firing quite different. The following year Ann and I decided to ride the Carol Train as passengers, and at Wharf I went to the front to greet the loco crew. The young man who was fireman said to me that he hoped that I didn't mind him doing my turn! This comment touched me deeply.

Having retired from Board and Council I was asked to become a Trustee of the Narrow Gauge Railway Museum, and this was during the run-up to the redevelopment of Wharf when a large amount of work would be required. I was able to assist Brian Owen in his task and he has produced for us the superb facility we now have, which is the envy of all those in the railway preservation field. Once the Museum was reopened I undertook to arrange regular working parties to carry out all the myriad of tasks that need to be done regularly such as keeping the place spick and span and carrying out improvements, etc. This work continues to this day and is an essential feature of Museum life. I also started the challenge of arranging for a trained volunteer to be a duty attendant whenever

On 28 August 2000 the TR celebrated the birthday of *Peter Sam*. Rev Wilbert Awdry, author of the very popular 'Thomas the Tank Engine' books, was a guard on the TR in the early days, and some of the stories about the 'Skarloey Railway' in the series were based on real happenings from his days as a guard. On the footplate is Fireman Tony Baker, and from left to right in front of the engine are Sue Whitehouse, Winston McCanna, Driver Bill Heynes, Jo Plumridge, Debbie Sharpe, Lis Mann (Duty Controller), Christopher Awdry (Wilbert's son), Eric Wooding and Adam Tams. *TR Collection*

Volunteers' stories

the Museum is open to the public, and although that task is now fulfilled by another I still take my place regularly on the Attendants Roster.

The Talyllyn has taken me to places I would never otherwise have gone and I have met a huge number of very interesting people. I have met Royalty on behalf of the TR twice, and that is something to be proud of. However, my most cherished side benefit was to receive an invitation to go to Australia for the opening of the Puffing Billy Railway's extension from Lakeside to Gembrooke. Unfortunately the invitation didn't include an air ticket, but the members out there very kindly found me accommodation and entertained me royally. I travelled out and back with Maurice Wilson, with whom I had worked so closely for so long and had become very good friends, and we had a trip to remember. Because of all the central roles I have fulfilled during these last 30 years I am known to many volunteers, both active and supportive. The problem is I can never hope to remember all of their names, so please forgive me for that.

Membership of the TRPS and being an active

Driver and Fireman stand in front of their engine and No 3 *Sir Haydn* in the loop at Wharf. *TR Collection*

volunteer has been one of the great joys to me and I can only feel sorry for members who do not take full advantage of what is on offer. To have had the distinction of being its Chairman for a period is a great honour, and in our 60-year history the number who have held that office can be counted on the fingers and toes of one person.

Ian Drummond

My first visit to the Talyllyn was a part of a family holiday in 1966. Being only eight at the time I don't remember too much about it, but it must have made an impression. A few years later I read Tom Rolt's *Railway Adventure*, which inspired me to want to visit again, so in 1972 we returned once more for a family holiday staying at Ynysmaengwyn, which was also part of my father's recuperation from serious illness. I remember walking down to the sheds at Pendre in the morning to watch the locos and carriages being prepared for the day, and wishing I could help. Sadly my father died in 1974, but my mother, seeing my enthusiasm for railways, encouraged me to get involved.

Ian Drummond. *Paul Gunn*

Living in Southampton, distance was an issue, but this is where the Wessex Area Group came in, and my first experience of volunteering for the railway was at its first model railway show, held in Winchester in 1975. Memories of that day are of it being extremely hot and crowded, but of being made to feel welcome. Part of the day I spent operating Jim Gadd's model of Rhydyronen to the delight of those watching. However, I was also entrusted with assisting Wilbert Awdry, helping to oversee books being autographed, etc.

From this event myself and my good friend Steve Hailes became increasing involved in the Wessex Group. Jim Gadd and his wife Pat were then responsible for the Group's sales stand, and we found ourselves travelling all over the area helping. Aiding us in this was George Voller, who willingly gave us lifts to all sorts of locations.

Memories of those days are many, including enduring the mud at the big traction engine show at Stourpaine Bushes, as well as being in the baking heat of the summer of 1976 at various events. A particular memory was of our taking the sales stand to the Isle of Wight Steam Shows over the August Bank Holiday starting in 1975, an event that was to later influence my career! It was all good fun, and gave the opportunity to raise some money for the railway, as well as generate publicity.

Another useful piece of publicity was doing window displays, initially in connection with the model railway shows, but later more widely. For this Steve and his father Bob built a small OO-gauge layout 'Farway', and our exhibition manager and electronics genius Bob Goodwin produced a system to operate the layout by means of photo-cells stuck to the inside of the window. To make the train operate children standing outside the window just had to cover one cell with their hand, the difference in light levels starting the train. We also discovered that at night you could make it work by shining a torch on one cell – something that attracted the attention of the local constabulary as we tested it out on a display in a building society window in Southampton one evening!

The model railway shows organised by the group were also a source of publicity and income. As has been mentioned, the first show at Winchester had been a great success, and it was felt that we should organise another, only this time at a larger venue. Steve and I realised that our school hall might provide a suitable place, so after some negotiation the Society's second exhibition was held there on 28 February 1976. Bob Goodwin, our exhibition manager, became very nervous about whether it would be a success, but in the end more than 3,700 people attended the one-day show! However, the following year, due to the fact that Southampton was playing Manchester United in a re-run of the previous

Guard Ian Drummond looks a bit worried as Fireman Matt Shield talks to his driver on No 2 Dolgoch, *standing in the west platform at Abergynolwyn in 2001. Judging by the smoke at the far end of the train, it appears that it is 'topped and tailed' for some reason.* TR Collection

Volunteers' stories

year's FA Cup Final at the team's ground, which was only half a mile from the school, numbers were down – we only got 2,700 that year! One more show was held at the school, until we moved, through the good offices of Bob Hailes, to the Mountbatten Theatre in the centre of the city, and from there to several venues, until they are now held in Fareham.

In the meantime my first experience of formally volunteering on the railway came in the summer of 1975. Particular memories of that week include our first encounter with Jan Cox (or 'Flower' as she was known); I think it has to be said that she was less than thrilled to discover that she had been rostered with two trainee guards on their first week on the railway. However, by the end of the day friendships were forged that lasted years. Then later that week we were given a guided tour by her husband John of the work that was being done on the then unfinished extension to Nant Gwernol.

The distances involved meant that we could only get to Tywyn about once a year, but they were memorable times even so. In 1976 the Nant Gwernol extension was opened, and a new timetable introduced. Passenger numbers also continued to climb, and there was talk of the need to operate a four train service to cope. People-packing became an art form in the summer peak weeks, with four, sometimes five aside on the seats. 'Children on laps please,' became a standard cry for guards. People were regularly conveyed in the guard's van on busy down trains, the record being taken by 'Flower', who managed 27 people in one, with her standing on the running board hanging on outside.

Steve and myself gradually climbed the

> One of the stalwarts of the TR for many years was the late Janet Cox. She was a Guard, Controller, Blockman, Booking Clerk and Training Officer for a number of years, then, quite late on in her TR career, she started working on the engines, first as a cleaner, and became known to all as 'Auntie Flower'. In 1985 and 1986 there were two occasions when she was firing an evening train, and here we see her in 1985 with Driver Viv Thorpe and Fireman Steve Powell in front of a banner put up by some volunteers to mark the fact that she was firing 'under supervision'. *Nigel Adams*

promotion ladder, but he was always ahead of me. In the early 1980s he was promoted to Guard while I was still an Assistant, and on one occasion we were rostered together on a train, a recipe for trouble! Dai Jones, whose family has been involved with the railway for years, was our driver for one trip. Dai had a wicked sense of humour, and obviously saw the opportunity to have some fun. Between us we made Steve's life miserable that trip.

At Nant Gwernol the tail lamp magically moved between the ends of the train twice. However, the high point came at Brynglas on the down trip. We stopped to exchange tokens, and Steve got out to supervise the train. Dai got my attention from the footplate, and beckoned me to climb out of the other side of the van and onto the engine. Here he stood me in the middle where Steve couldn't see me. Steve gave the 'right away', and leapt back into the van, only to realise I wasn't there. It took him several minutes trying to figure where I'd gone; meanwhile we were having a great time on the loco just watching the expression on his face!

Of course those years were ones of many changes in our lives – university, and beginning a career. I made the wise decision to marry Di, who shares my interest in railways, being a railway historian with an international reputation in her own right. However, even though I had by now been promoted to guard, and was involved in the Wessex Group while we lived in the area, for a number of reasons I did not volunteer on the railway for nine years.

It was not until 1992 that I returned to volunteering at Tywyn following a conversation with John Smallwood, when we visited the line on a day trip. However, because of the length of time I had been away it was decided that I needed at least one day as an assistant guard to refamiliarise myself with the job. My Guard for the day was Nigel Adams, who informed me, as we pulled away from Wharf on our first up trip, 'By the way, I'm now an Anglican vicar.'

'That's all right,' I replied, 'I'm now a Baptist minister.'

And with that the 'Ecumenical Express' charged up the line.

Well, the years have gone on, and I have got much pleasure from volunteering on the Talyllyn. Both my 40th and 50th birthdays were celebrated with trips to the railway for a day's guarding. I was greatly honoured to be asked to preach at the 50th Anniversary service for the Preservation Society, although I think my blowing a whistle to start the sermon didn't please everybody!

Now I suppose I am one of the 'senior

Ian was one of several ordained TR volunteers. The late Phil Guest was driving a train one day in 1989 and remarked that it needed a 'Rev counter' on it as both the Driver, Malcolm Brown, and the Guard, Nigel Adams, were priests in the Anglican church. In their layover at Wharf they therefore made a 'Rev counter', which was a large piece of white card with the words 'Rev Counter – 2' on it; this was tied to the loco lamp so that Phil Guest could see it when his train crossed theirs at Brynglas. Here Malcolm and Nigel stand on No 3 *Sir Haydn* at Nant Gwernol alongside the sign. *Nigel Adams collection*

Volunteers' stories

volunteers' theoretically transferring their wisdom to the next generation, and indeed it does give me great pleasure to see new volunteers come to the railway, particularly the youngsters, reminding me of what it was like for me in those early years. The vast majority have been a great delight to work with, and its been a pleasure to see them go on and make a success of their life on the railway and beyond. There are still many friends around from those early days, too many to mention, although sadly some are no longer with us. But I know they would be delighted to see the way the railway continues to preserve the spirit of the Talyllyn, and will hopefully do so for many years to come.

The Young family: Gerry, Helen, Simon and Andrew

We first visited the Talyllyn Railway in 1979, during a family holiday in Fairbourne. It was a big adventure when we drove down to Tywyn, had lunch at a cafe in the High Street, then went to find the railway. Gerry knew about the TR already, so it seemed an opportunity not to be missed to pay it a visit. It was a rather grey day, but there is a photo of us sitting in one of the open coaches, so the weather couldn't have been too bad. As we rode up the line we spotted the Tynllwyn caravan site, so made up our minds to camp there the following summer.

We stayed at Tynllwyn for a number of years, and gradually got involved with the TR. First we became members (the offer of free travel was a big inducement there!), then became involved with the East Midlands Area Group where Gerry became the Stockholder for about ten years. At the time Liz Green ran the railway shop, and we asked her one day if there was any way we could volunteer as a family with two young boys. As a result the Dolgoch trolley was dusted off, and we spent a few days at Dolgoch each summer selling chocolate bars and soft drinks to passengers. If the boys got bored, one of us could amuse them with a walk up to the Falls or a ride on a train.

We used to chat to the station staff, and one day the young lady in charge asked Simon (then aged 12) if he would like to accompany her as an 'unofficial trainee' on her guarding duty the following day. The lower age limit was not so

Gerry Young.

strictly enforced in those days! He thoroughly enjoyed his day on the train, and I (Helen) seem to remember that he spent another day or two in similar fashion that summer. Within a year or two he and Gerry were volunteering for most of our holiday, leaving Andrew and me to amuse ourselves. As Andrew wanted to work on the locos, he had to wait until he was 14 – the age limit was enforced more rigidly there.

The two of us still took the trolley to Dolgoch occasionally, and generally helped in the shop in any way we could. I remember Andrew selling 'Talyllyn 125' commemorative newspapers on the platform at Wharf. Eventually in 1991 he reached the age of 14, and could be let loose on the engines. That left yours truly to help in the shop and cafe, then at the craft fairs during 'Victorian Week' and beyond. I also did a few station duties, but not enough to warrant a grade card.

When the boys were teenagers, we used to come to Tywyn occasionally for Area Group outdoor working parties. We soon discovered that the winter weather could be somewhat inclement. Then, when the boys were off our hands, Gerry joined the gang of 'bodgers'. He enjoys working on the coaches, and the temperature in the paint shop in winter was more to his liking. I was again left twiddling my fingers – the shop and cafe were too quiet to need any help. Then I noticed the sad state of the upholstery in the coaches; nobody had done any work on the seats in years. So I have replaced foam and made new covers for almost all the seats in the coaches, and even sewn a batch of antimacassars for the 1st Class.

Simon received his Guard's grade card on his last day of volunteering before he went to university, but has been too busy to make use of it since. His only appearances in Tywyn recently have been for Race the Train, but there are usually a few people who still recognise him. His absence is made up for by his brother Andrew, who is a fixture on the Talyllyn.

Helen Young with Simon and Andrew in pre-volunteering days!

Volunteers' stories

Guard Simon Young.

Andrew Young

My earliest memories of the Talyllyn Railway are of summer holidays as a child spent camping at Tynllwyn and running to the gate to wave at the passing trains. On the campsite we soon got to know other children whose parents were volunteers, so getting involved was fairly inevitable! After a few years of riding on the railway as passengers as part of our holiday, we started volunteering as a family by taking a refreshment trolley up to Dolgoch. My Dad and brother Simon started volunteering in the Traffic Department, while I was more attracted to the Loco Department, but waiting to turn 14 seemed to take for ever! One day the track gang were having lunch at Dolgoch and one of their members, a kindly gentleman by the name of Iolo Davies, took pity on me and invited me to spend the following day out on the gang with them. I'm not sure quite what use a 12-year-old boy was as a look-out while the gang was strimming back lineside vegetation near Brynglas, but I was hooked. The following summer was spent helping shop manageress Liz Green, mainly selling guide books and 'Talyllyn 125' newspapers to passengers as they waited to depart from Wharf, and using my 'cuteness' to advantage to maximise sales, something I couldn't rely on today! Riding up the valley on some days and a couple of illicit rides on the loco back from Nant Gwernol to Abergynolwyn confirmed that it was the Loco Department for me.

My 14th birthday eventually arrived and during the Spring Bank Holiday of 1991 I got my wish and started in the Loco Department. Several happy summer holidays were spent transferring dirt from the locos onto myself and receiving an education of a kind that school didn't provide! In the intervening 20 years I have been lucky to have been able to put the time in and progress through the grades, and I am now 'let loose' as a Driver.

While the Talyllyn changes very little through time, the people who volunteer on the railway

Andrew Young on the footplate, then and now!

have done. Over those 20 years (and I'm still a youngster!) people have come and gone, some to return in later life with their children, others to retire, while some are sadly no longer with us. Those with whom I first worked had often been involved since the early days and had some fantastic stories to tell; thankfully a lot of them have been published in the *Talyllyn News* and elsewhere to live on for the next generation. Nowadays there are more people rostered to drive on the Talyllyn, but when I started the turns were divided among far fewer people. A lot of driving was done by two people, Maurice Wilson and Roy Smith. I cleaned for Maurice on many occasions. I remember sharing No 2's tank top in the cab with his posters and paste bucket, as Maurice would spend his tea breaks attending to the posters up the line – and woe betide any cleaner who overfilled No 2's tank and got them sodden at the start of the day! On a hot day Maurice liked to swap his grease-top for a flat cap when out on the line between stations; there was much entertainment for the fireman and cleaner on the occasions when Maurice would realise he still had his flat cap on when arriving at a station with people taking photos, and the quick change into his grease-top was often accompanied by a banging of his head on the low cab roof on the way in, and sometimes on the way out of the cab! I was lucky enough to fire to Maurice a few times as a Passed Cleaner before he retired, by which time he'd swapped his allegiance to No 7.

On one occasion the token machines had failed and we'd travelled from Brynglas to Quarry Siding on a T22 paper ticket. Approaching

Volunteers' stories

'Let's have a break!' Brenda Jones (who worked in the cafe at the time), the late Don Southgate (then the TR Signal & Telegraph Engineer), an unknown person and Roy Smith enjoy a break and a chat outside the cafe, which at that time was a temporary structure at the far end of Wharf platform. It served the TR well for many years. *TR Collection*

Quarry we both looked at the empty token rack, then at each other, and were completely horror-stricken for a moment until we remembered that the ticket was in Maurice's pocket! I spent less time cleaning and firing to Roy Smith, but when I did it was invariably on No 1. To this day, being rostered on No 1 feels a bit like being allowed to take Roy's engine out! Trips up the valley with Roy were always filled with stories and anecdotes, normally with an educational aspect to them; I first learned of the Abermule accident through a trip with Roy, and the lessons it taught in terms of operating railways. David Ratcliff was always the consummate gentleman and was the first to allow me as a fireman to drive a round trip. This caused some ructions amongst the establishment as I was only in my first year as a fireman. But David was always keen to encourage younger volunteers and wasn't afraid to stand up to authority!

I spent quite a bit of time firing to Phil Guest, definitely a case of every day being a school day. Phil taught me that, as long as you carry out your duties in a safe manner, the second most important aspect is to enjoy yourself in the process. Phil was keen to stress the importance of teamwork between the driver, the fireman and the guard. He also introduced me to the world of 'Harry Potter' books, not quite what you might expect from a tea break while firing to a retired teacher! One of Phil's notable traits when all was going well on the loco was to eat an orange

Written on the back of this photo is 'Thank you for a lovely day – David and Karen Rowe'. This is the comment TR volunteers love to hear and do so often, making it all worthwhile. David Rowe stands with the Driver, the late Phil Guest, who taught Maths at a school in Wolverhampton and introduced Andrew to the 'Harry Potter' books. *TR Collection*

going down the valley. The pips were invariably discarded at the bottom of Cynfal bank, leading to suggestions that planting an orange grove there would be a suitable tribute. Later, after I passed out for driving and Phil came along to inspect me, there waiting on the coat hook in the cab to greet him was a net of clementines.

One essential ingredient of a railway's operation is tea, or, more correctly, the drinking of copious quantities of the stuff! Today Pendre tea is very much of a likeness with that found in everyday life. When I first started, Pendre tea was a delicacy hitherto unknown to the wider world and something that I was soon to discover. Shortly before 10.30 in the morning and 3.30 in the afternoon, one of the cleaners would stop what he was doing and venture to the mess room and charge the kettles. Once the pot was warmed, he would carefully measure out the tea leaves into the pot (provide the staff with weak tea and you were in trouble!) make the tea, shout 'Tea up!' into the works and down the phone to whoever answered in the distant reaches of Pendre, pour a mug-full, add the desired quantity of powdered milk and sugar to taste (to date this has been the only time I've ever had sugar in tea!) and find a seat by the stove if wet, or the platform. Pendre tea was definitely an acquired taste (a bit like draught Bass in the Corbett, after being told it was better for me than Cola!), and to date I've yet to find anything comparable in taste; the closest would be the chai served on the trains in India.

The opening of 'Llechfan' hostel coincided with me turning 16 and being able to be in Tywyn on my own without parents. Having the hostel is one of the biggest advantages for the Talyllyn to encourage younger volunteers to make the journey to Tywyn. This led to me spending my university holidays in Tywyn, working as a barman in the Corbett and latterly the Whitehall when the TR custom moved across the road. Spending long summers in Tywyn led me to join the Traffic Department, as the number of turns on the locos was limited. In two summers I became a guard and a blockman. One memory is of working the lunchtime shift in the Corbett, swapping my bow-tie for a Talyllyn tie, guarding the 1610 turn, swapping back to a bow-tie and heading back to the Corbett to work the evening shift! Although in the main I prefer to spend my time on the locos, I can still be found occasionally enjoying a peaceful day blocking or, even rarer, the odd guarding turn or two.

One day Don Southgate asked me whether I'd consider becoming a Signalling Inspector. He reckoned that by spending a lot of time on the footplate, I'd be in the ideal place to keep an eye on blockmen without them realising it! This has worked well and it amazes me how some blockmen get stressed by the prospect of a Signalling Inspector in their blockpost, yet are very relaxed when I'm standing outside their blockpost having stepped off a loco. So maybe Don was right after all!

After university the Talyllyn played an important part in my career choice because I had no idea as to what I wanted to do. My parents were suggesting that I find a proper job after graduating, so naturally I took their advice and accepted the offer of a summer job driving on the Fairbourne Railway! An entertaining summer resulted, and I am reminded of some of the more entertaining aspects from time to time. Finally, after months of part-time work and rejected job applications, the Talyllyn connection came in handy and got me an interview for a clerical position with Virgin Trains. I had intended to keep my footplate ambitions to the Talyllyn; however, after two years of clerical work I felt the need to escape from working in an office and got a job driving at Virgin's CrossCountry depot at Derby. Writing this 12 years after joining the 'big railway', I have no regrets about my career choice and I am grateful to the Talyllyn for its input into me doing what I enjoy doing now. To top it all off, during my initial driver training at Polmadie in Glasgow one of the locos I got to drive was electric loco No 86258, the other *Talyllyn*.

One aspect of the TR I enjoy is the ability to put in as much or as little as you want to, or are able to. I enjoy, and am lucky to spend the time doing, a variety of jobs. Although the locos will always come first for me, guarding and blocking helps to give a different perspective to the railway.

My parents first introduced me to the Talyllyn in the winter through taking part in East Midlands Area Group working parties, working on projects in the museum and any outdoor jobs that needed doing. Graham White was loco working party organiser at the time and went round with his notebook asking which working party dates you could attend. This led to me travelling down to Tywyn with my parents and spending the weekends up at Pendre. Seeing the locos stripped down into their components was an eye-opener for me, more used to writing essays

Volunteers' stories

and reports at college, and helped me understand how they worked. Since then I have continued to get to Pendre when I can to help out, doing whatever jobs the Chief Engineer has for me. Turning a drawing into a finished product is quite rewarding, especially for someone whose day job is completely different.

However, there is plenty of variety to be had at Pendre if you're happy to do whatever's needed. My last few visits before writing this have included helping out with winter loco maintenance, constructing a trolley for the outdoor gang, helping dismantle the Nant Gwernol footbridge and digging holes to be filled with concrete. The Talyllyn Railway Preservation Society is an incredibly democratic body and the option is there for those who wish to partake in the committee structure. Having tried it and found it not to my liking, I have returned to putting my energies to better use elsewhere. One task I did enjoy tremendously was spending five years as editor of the 'Talyllyn Volunteer' newsletter.

One thing the Talyllyn has taught me in the time I've been involved, and hopefully will continue to in coming years, is that fellow volunteers become almost like a second family to you – there to celebrate the good times and support you through the bad times. A special community indeed.

In May 2001 Virgin electric loco No 86258 was named *Talyllyn* at Birmingham International station, with the 'real' *Talyllyn* alongside it. This picture shows Nigel Adams (who blessed the loco) holding the duplicate nameplate (which is on display at Wharf station) together with Peter Bowes, Ian Davies and Roger Whitehouse, who was Chairman of the TRPS at that time. Peter Bowes and Ian Davies were there in two capacities, as senior managers of Virgin CrossCountry and as TR volunteers. The Virgin Town Crier was also there in his official capacity. *TR Collection*

Anthony Coulls

Looking back over my 37 years, I find it amazing that the TR has been part of life for 26 of them – that's longer than I've been at work, longer than I've been married. In fact, the only longer constants have been my parents and my sister, all of whom have had a degree of involvement with the Talyllyn Railway at one stage or another.

I first met the Talyllyn when I was three, though I don't recall much. One of my teachers at school, Mrs Foster, had a husband who was a volunteer on the railway, but with family at Talybont, near Harlech, most early holiday railway memories are of the Fairbourne Railway and the Festiniog. That changed in 1982 when we visited the Talyllyn, and I recall a red *Sir Handel*, which of course was No 3 in Awdry guise. Three years later, as a member of the British Rail-sponsored 'Rail Riders' club, there was an offer for junior membership of the TRPS – and I joined. I sometimes wonder how many others who joined around the same time are still members?

We still kept visiting during holidays, but in 1988 I had a taste of working as a volunteer on the Ravenglass & Eskdale Railway, which led to me becoming a Severn Valley Railway working member. I don't remember how it happened, but in the spring of 1990 my parents asked me, 'Which railway would you like to volunteer on – the Severn Valley or the Talyllyn?' I opted for the latter! Mrs Foster's husband was active in the Loco Department and also a member of the model railway club in Leamington of which I was a member. Upon hearing that I was going to Tywyn that summer he told me that he would speak to his friend Maurice Wilson, who would look after me. So it was in July 1990 that I joined the Loco Department for two weeks – but by the end of it, I knew I would be back. People such as Perry Price, John Nixon and Richard Davis shared their experience with me, and I often think back to them all and wonder where they are now. Of course, many of the Talyllyn family we still know to this day, and some who have now passed on became familiar and, in many cases, friends. Some of our younger drivers hadn't even started as volunteers then!

My involvement with the Severn Valley tailed off in 1991, and we began to spend every school holiday – half-terms, Easter and summer – at Tywyn. I finished school in 1992, then had four weeks that summer on the railway, as well as the Easter and half-term holidays and working a Santa Special weekend. A special moment came in March that year when, for my 18th birthday, I received life membership of the TRPS.

By very great fortune, in September 1992 I started university at Aberystwyth, only 35 miles by road or rail from Tywyn. Suffice it to say that on Friday nights and Sunday afternoons I became well acquainted with either the buses or the waiting room at Machynlleth station, as a late-running connection meant a long pause there on the journey to Tywyn.

Anthony Coulls.

Volunteers' stories

The TR is not all work, and there are good social events. On this occasion a double-decker bus was hired for an event, and Anthony is seen in the front seat upstairs.
TR Collection

I retained an involvement in the Loco Department as in 1992 I was promoted to Passed Cleaner, but I found enjoyment working in the outdoor gangs too, from sorting rails to digging out Cynfal Bank when it flooded and blocked the line just before a Santa train weekend. I enjoyed being part of the Tywyn Area Group, and went to socials and dinners, and assisted with sales at model railway events and such like. We chartered special trains for the Aberystwyth University Railway & Transport Society and I was fortunate enough to be able to fire those trips, and the Talyllyn magic rubbed off on a few of my colleagues from the university, some of whom are active to this day. The TR has a special magic socially, too, of course, and I have fond memories of bus trips to the Ffestiniog and Bala railways, together with Young Members' Group socials, New Year parties, and of course parties for no better reason than they were fun.

We did daft things like push a carriage to Nant Gwernol in 1994, drive a traction engine round Tywyn for TR publicity (allegedly) and did our best to inject humour into AGM Day train services and other events (anyone remember No 9 with a blue flashing police light on it?). I joined the Museum & Heritage Committee and later got all grown up when I was elected a Trustee of the Narrow Gauge Railway Museum. I took Kathryn, my then girlfriend, to the railway, and she had a footplate ride. She then became my fiancée and had a trip on the engine with Phil Guest and myself, and, as my wife, is now a longstanding member together with our two daughters. In more recent times we were heavily involved in running the Tom Rolt Steam & Vintage Rally from 2003 to 2008, which was our way of supporting the TR from afar, as with two little girls the practicalities of working on the railway didn't work out. Since 2008 I have been fortunate to make a semi-comeback and spend time on the footplate again, which has been great fun.

Many long friendships were made in those early years, and it gave me much pleasure in 2002 to have one of my longest TR friends, John Smallwood, as the best man at my wedding. Sadly some folk have gone, and I count it a privilege to have known David Ratcliff, Don Southgate, Phil Guest, Graham Jenkins, Tony Bennett and Maurice Wilson among others, but it is invidious to mention too many names from such a long time period. A measure of the depth of the TR friendship is when relationships pick up after sometimes several years away or apart. In my case, this has been especially true – as the 1990s progressed, my career moved me further away from Tywyn, culminating in me writing these words from County Durham. The time I am able to give to the Talyllyn these days is far less than it used to be, with the demands of a young family and a busy job, but it has always been wonderful to see TR friends both in Tywyn and across the country and chat as if no time has passed at all. A further example of the extended TR family was when we moved up to the North East and I was shopping in the local Tesco wearing a Talyllyn fleece and a voice said, 'It's Anthony Coulls, isn't it?' The voice belonged to Andrew Jordan, a fellow Loco Department volunteer and friend from my earlier times whom I'd not seen for nearly 10 years – and we are now back in regular contact, and back on the TR as footplate crew again.

I have been fortunate enough to make railway preservation my career, now working as Senior Curator of Rail Vehicle Collections for the National Railway Museum, but my first love was, is and always will be the Talyllyn – it has been part of me for far longer, and I will always be the same person as the 16-year-old I was who set foot in Pendre that first time back in 1990. I may never make it to driver, as the 18-year-old me once hoped, but the Talyllyn and I are inseparable. Long may it continue.

Andrew Robinson

2001 was an important year in the Talyllyn Railway's long and varied history. It marked 50 years since a group of enthusiastic amateurs had taken over the running of the line, and in the process kick-started railway preservation. But 2001 will always have a more important personal significance to me, as it was the year I realised my dream of volunteering on the Talyllyn and starting my footplate career. Little did I realise, however, that there would be much, much more to my involvement with the TR than just cleaning steam engines.

Like many youngsters, my interest in trains stemmed from a childhood spent watching episodes of 'Thomas the Tank Engine' and reading the Rev'd Awdry's classic books. Over time, this evolved into a love of 'real' steam trains. As I got older I became aware that the preserved lines I enjoyed visiting were run by volunteers. The idea that I too could help run a railway was almost too good to be true, and I began looking forward to the day when I would be old enough to join a preservation society.

Coming from the West Country (and being a disciple of all things Swindon), it seemed inevitable that I would end up joining one of my local lines like the West Somerset or the South Devon. However, reading all those 'Thomas' books as a youngster had made me aware of a line in Wales called the Talyllyn Railway. I was intrigued by the thought of a real railway so like the ones on the Island of Sodor, so when we went on a family holiday to Wales I was determined that we should visit it.

From the moment I saw it I was hooked. It was early spring and the trees were still bare as my family and I climbed the steep path to Dolgoch station, nestling among the trees and deserted. All was quiet except for the gurgle of water from the

Andrew Robinson

Volunteers' stories

Two schoolboys are captivated by No 4 *Edward Thomas* taking water at Dolgoch Falls (probably in 1953, judging from the headboard), just as Andrew had been on a spring day nearly 50 years later. *TR Collection*

stream feeding the sturdy slate water tower and the distant bleating of sheep. All of a sudden it began to snow heavily, and just then, with a shrill whistle of warning, a small red engine puffed into view around the corner, hauling a neat rake of coaches. For me, it was a magical moment.

I was immediately charmed by the bustling little engines and the beautiful scenery of the Fathew Valley. But what became clear over the course of subsequent visits was how very friendly the people running the railway were. All the staff had time to stop and chat and were only too glad to invite you onto the footplate or into their signal box. If, I reasoned, I was going to volunteer anywhere, surely this would be an ideal place to start?

And so it proved. On my first weekend volunteering I was welcomed with open arms. Without exception, everyone was friendly and helpful. Even though I was young and inexperienced, I soon felt part of 'the gang'. It didn't matter that I was still at school, that I didn't know how to operate a token machine, nor had the foggiest idea how an air pump worked. What mattered was that I was there because of a love of the Talyllyn, that I was prepared to do my bit, and that I was enthusiastic. And boy, was I enthusiastic! That weekend I coaled and watered engines, pulled points, pushed trucks, polished brass, and generally felt that I couldn't possibly be more involved in the running of the railway. Looking back, I was only scratching the surface, but at the time I was delighted to be so 'hands on'. During that first visit I was also pleasantly surprised to find a number of other youngsters, both male and female, at work on the railway. It was something of a revelation to find so many people of my own age who shared my interests, and it was the start of my introduction to the vibrant social life of the railway, which rapidly became just as important and as enjoyable as actually volunteering. It's good fun to be able to spend the day indulging your hobby; it's even more fun to do it with a bunch of mates.

As time went by I gained more experience and progressed through the ranks of the Loco Department. I remember waiting eagerly for the day when I would get my first solo firing turn. I used to imagine some crisis situation in which I was the only person available to fire a train, and rose magnificently to the occasion. Then one day it happened! I was cleaning out the ash pit when Bill Heynes, the Duty Shedman, came up to me.

'Go and get changed – you're going out firing,' he said.

It transpired that the fireman on *Sir Haydn* that day had hurt his knee and required relief. However, the Spare Fireman had already had to go out on one of the other engines, and I was the only person left to step into the breach. I wouldn't say I 'rose magnificently to the occasion', but I did a fair job of firing No 3 and felt that I was really starting to get somewhere. I've had many firing turns since then, but none have been quite as exciting!

At that time Wharf station was being rebuilt. It was a trying time, with short platform working, involving much propelling backwards and forwards between Wharf and Pendre, as well as some tight turn-rounds, but everyone rose to the occasion. We would often be held at the Wharf home signal while the station staff closed the chains that protected the level crossing during that period. When that happened, the fireman would have to hop off and use the phone provided to call the station and remind them of his train's presence. However, it seemed to always be the case that as soon as you got to the phone (which was often surrounded by mud) the signal would clear. It happened so often that many of us began to think it was happening on purpose; one fireman suggested that the station staff had rigged up a hidden camera so they would know just when to change it!

When the new building was complete, Their Royal Highnesses the Prince of Wales and the Duchess of Cornwall came to perform the official opening. It was a busy day, and once the locos had gone off shed in the morning I and another cleaner, Andrew Thomas, were left alone at Pendre. When the Royal Train arrived, Prince Charles was to alight and get on the footplate of *Tom Rolt* for the short trip down to Wharf. Andrew and I thought we might as well have a look at our special visitor, so we smartened ourselves up and waited on the platform. The train duly arrived and down stepped Prince Charles, who was ushered towards the engine. Imagine our surprise when he stopped to shake hands and have a chat with us! We weren't on the list of people he was to meet officially as part of his visit, so we were a little taken aback. He came across as friendly and knowledgeable, however, although he never did take me up on my suggestion that he spend a week with the track gang during winter Outdoor Week…

Talking of outdoor work reminds me of the time we tackled the relaying of the Wharf

Andrew, firing on No 2 *Dolgoch*, is ready to leave Wharf station. *Andrew Robinson collection*

Volunteers' stories

Edge siding as a New Year project. Part of the work involved reinstalling one of the old wagon turntables. When it was in place, we naturally got talking about giving it a test. The trouble was, what could we turn on it? Most of the trucks we had down at Wharf were too long. Then someone mentioned that *Midlander* might just be small enough… A plan was hatched. Once it was dark, a group of us headed up to Pendre and extracted No 5 from among a row of trucks. It hadn't been used for a while, but we got it started and trundled down to Wharf. As quietly as we could (which was not very), we ran No 5 round to the turntable and, with much heaving and shoving, managed to turn it through 180 degrees. We then hurried back to Pendre as quickly as we could, before any of the 'great and the good', who were having a meeting in the cafe, could notice. We parked *Midlander* back exactly where it had been amongst the trucks without anyone being any the wiser. I gather it was about a week before any on the staff noticed that No 5 was the wrong way round… To me, that story epitomises what working on the Talyllyn is like. We work hard and get the job done, but we play hard too and know how to enjoy ourselves. It is the enjoyment in the work, the sense of satisfaction I get from doing it, and the friendship of those I work with that has kept me coming back for more than a decade now.

Andrew uses the old water tower and wooden chute at Dolgoch Falls station to water No 2 *Dolgoch*. *Andrew Robinson collection*

The Talyllyn is much more than just a railway – it is like a big extended family. I have made lifelong friends through volunteering there. I met my girlfriend there. It may even have helped me get my current job. Not content with being an 'amateur' railwayman, I've now gone professional and work for Network Rail. I can't help wondering if having all that TR experience on my CV may have helped swing things in my favour. But whether it did or not, the Talyllyn has undoubtedly had a big impact on my life. It has given me a wealth of experience, opportunity, fun and, above all, friendship. I hope it will continue to do so for many years to come.

No 5 *Midlander* at Wharf station. *D. J. Mitchell*

Matthew Wear

2011 is my tenth year as a volunteer. I mainly volunteer in the Traffic Department acting as Guard, Blockman, Booking Clerk, Station Master and Controller. I am also the Training Coordinator for the railway and am responsible for organising training for the specific grades of volunteers during the season. I am also a member of the TRPS Council and am currently the Minutes Secretary for Council, which involves preparing the papers for the meetings, taking the minutes and providing various reports following the meeting. I also sit on the Traffic & Operating, Finance & General Purposes committees, together with the Marketing & Strategic Committee.

My family have always taken holidays in Tywyn and owned a static caravan for much of my childhood, and it was during that time that I discovered the Talyllyn Railway. I travelled on the railway day after day as a young lad, going for walks and spending time watching and learning what was done on and around it. During this time of travelling I made many friends with the volunteers who were very encouraging and supportive in getting me to become a volunteer, which I did when I was 15. Taking the initial step was a bit scary as I was suddenly moving from being an ordinary passenger travelling up and down the line to someone who was actually helping to give the passengers an enjoyable experience and keep the railway working.

When I joined the railway as a volunteer I started out as a trainee guard learning the basic duties involved with guarding the train and gaining a general understanding of how the railway operated and how each person, contributing in their various ways, kept the whole thing together. From this I progressed to an assistant guard, which allowed me to guard trains under the direct supervision of the Guard; this gave me not only increased responsibility but also an understanding of what it was like to be in charge of the train. During my time as an assistant guard I also undertook duties as station master along the line, helping people on and off the trains and selling tickets to new passengers

Matthew Wear.

joining the train for the first time. Station duties are a lovely way of interacting with the passengers.

Another interest of mine was the role of the blockman (or signalman), and at the age of 16 I began my training, which involved shadowing various blockmen at the various blockposts along the line. As I gained experience I was able to perform the crossing of trains under the supervision of the blockman.

My next chapter was to qualify as a Passed Assistant Guard followed by Guard, then Blockman. I am now a regular volunteer in these grades and they give me great pleasure in ensuring the visitors to our railway have an enjoyable experience. I started to train to become a controller at the age of 18 and was very lucky to be able to act as a controller in my own right on my 21st birthday. During my time as a trainee controller I had some interesting experiences to deal with, including a locomotive failure that required a rescue and the re-pathing of the afternoon train service due to the late running that this caused. I also had to call out the emergency services for some medical emergencies with people managing to injure themselves while out walking. One of the great things about a lot of the volunteers is that we are 'multi-graded', so one day you can be the Controller, leading the team of volunteers for the day to ensure everything is done correctly and the service is provided, and another day you are Station Master at Rhydyronen seeing a train every 40 minutes with plenty of time to sit out in the sunshine and catch up with your book!

My role as Training Coordinator involves organising training weekends with simulated incidents for the various grades of volunteers, together with Mutual Improvement Classes during the main school holiday periods, where people of all grades come together for a couple of hours to talk and learn about a specific topic. I find this role very rewarding, and many of the volunteers enjoy the opportunity to experience incidents and situations that are not witnessed around the railway during the ordinary operating season.

The TR has a great social life and the volunteers ensure that everyone has a good time when they are working on it. During the main holiday periods there are members' barbecue trains and themed nights out, as well as meetings in the evening for a drink in the local pubs in the town.

The Talyllyn Railway is a major part of my life and I am so pleased that I got involved. It operates like a huge family and everyone rallies around to support each other in times of need, as I recently experienced when I suffered a nasty injury to my leg and foot. There are jobs for people from all walks of life and you do not need any experience to volunteer. On-the-job training is given and people will help and support you throughout.

In 2011 the Talyllyn Railway celebrated its 60th Anniversary, and what a year of celebration we had. Please tell you friends about our marvellous railway – you will always be made welcome and you can be part of it all. If you are interested please ask a member of staff on duty who will be happy to help you.

I made the big step, so why don't you?

Andrew Simner

I have been volunteering on the Talyllyn Railway since I was less than five years old! Like most people my age, we can blame our involvement with the Talyllyn on our fathers; mine found the railway while on a holiday staying near the line and was greeted by a friendly volunteer one day on a rainy platform, having just missed the train. My father's love for the railway was inflicted on my mother, and a year hasn't passed without a visit to the Talyllyn. What can a five-year-old do to contribute to the world's first preserved railway? I joined the band of young volunteers called 'Tracksiders', and for about ten years I worked with my friends under the supervision of my parents to rebuild slate fences, build the viewing platform near Dolgoch station, and the Adventure Playground at Abergynolwyn. The 'Tracksiders' was a social group for the children and their parents and it maintained my close link with the Talyllyn until I was 14 years old and responsible enough to volunteer in the Traffic Department as a trainee guard.

Andrew Simner.

Volunteers of all shapes and sizes are essential in keeping the Talyllyn steaming, and all the historic skills are taught to you on the job right from the start. On my first day I was met in the carriage shed 2 hours before the first train of the day, plenty of time to prepare the carriages for the first passengers. Even though I was a familiar face on the railway, having worked as a 'Tracksider', there were lots of things to learn about how the day-to-day operating staff went about their duties. I loved my time as a trainee, then as assistant guard, because I got to work alongside plenty of different adults of all ages and backgrounds. They taught me how to look after passengers and sell tickets, and when I was 18 I was old enough to guard the trains by myself. I now enjoy training others and am always really excited to see trainees coming through the ranks – it's not too long ago that I was in their shoes.

I've recently started taking advantage of all the different opportunities on offer at the Talyllyn: volunteering in the cafe, joining the working parties and spending time at the dirty end by cleaning and learning to fire the traditional steam engines. My proudest achievement, however, was during my two years as Secretary to the Young Members Group Committee; the Talyllyn is perhaps unique in the proportion of its volunteers who are under 25 years old. There is a real community among the young volunteers, especially in the volunteer hostel 'Llechfan', which is a cheap and sociable place to stay while volunteering, and convenient too, situated just across the tracks at Wharf station. In 2010 I organised a Young Volunteers Day, where we showcased our contribution and invited ordinary passengers to have a go at driving the engines, diesels and taking tours of the workshops. I want to share my enjoyment of the Talyllyn with others, and I always took advantage of opportunities at school to make presentations and persuade my friends to come all the way from Nottingham to volunteer in our half-term holidays, weekends and the luxuriously long summer break!

Some of my funniest memories of volunteering come from my school days; I remember working as the Station Master at Abergynolwyn station and being surprised that the next person to appear was my maths teacher from back home. As the years went by I learned which of my teachers were secret train fans and took full advantage. My 18th birthday, spent guarding my first train, was secured in return for a footplate ride for my Deputy Headmaster; I think that we both came out of that deal reasonably well!

I am not attracted to volunteering at the Talyllyn because of my love of trains; in all honesty I don't know one end of a steam engine from the other. However, that certainly doesn't put me off. The great friends I have made and the amazing community spirit on the railway mean that I could never leave, and I'm sure that in the future I will in turn inflict it on my children and hope to share all the very special experiences that I have had.

Jim Elliott

In September 2007 I decided to spend a few days in Wales to rediscover the Welsh narrow gauge railways, it having been more than 30 years since I had last visited them. A day was spent on the Corris, the Ffestiniog, the Welsh Highland, the Vale of Rheidol and the Talyllyn. Having enjoyed the visit so much I decided to go back for a few days the following May. This time I spent a couple of days on the TR, and did not know then what it would lead to. I have friends who volunteer on the Welsh Highland and Ffestiniog, and talking to them I realised the fun they were having on the railways. The decision was made to join one of the railway societies, but which one? The FR and WHR are wonderful railways, but there seemed to me to be an air of commercialism when visiting them. The Corris is another very good little line, but has a long way to go and seems to rely very heavily financially on the members.

I then started to think about the Talyllyn and remembered the very friendly atmosphere that greeted me when I walked out onto the platform at Wharf station. Nobody was in a hurry and

Volunteers' stories

Early 'bodging' days: restoring one of the original four coaches at Pendre. TR Collection

always had time to talk and answer questions. I also remembered to most enjoyable ride I had on the 'Victorian Train' the previous September. It was no contest – the Talyllyn it was, so in June 2008 I duly sent off my subscription to join the TRPS. The latest copy of the *Talyllyn News* arrived, which was read from cover to cover to find out exactly what I had joined. When I joined, getting involved by volunteering had not been the main object, but it was beginning to look like a good idea, but what to do? I read about the activities of the 'bodgers', which rather appealed to me. Being an engineer, I wanted to do something totally different, and carriage repairs looked to be just the job. I made another visit in September and had a chat with John Burton, Carriage Foreman and Chief Bodger, to find out more, and decided to become a 'bodger'.

During the winter I made four visits to the TR on 'bodging weekends' and thoroughly enjoyed myself. I found myself helping to replace floorboards and support timbers in an open carriage, replacing seat backs, repairing drop lights, etc, sorting out all the 'wear and tear' from the summer and meeting very friendly and helpful members at the same time – a wonderful way to spend a weekend. The Welsh weather can sometimes be unpredictable and the attraction of the warmth of the paint shop in midwinter made 'bodging' even more appealing. At the March weekend, a guard was needed for Mothering Sunday services, so John Burton was volunteered to guard for the day. He asked if I would like to spend the day with him in the brake-van to get some idea how the railway runs. It was a very good day, but TR brake-vans are not the warmest places on a cold March day. In June I arranged with John to have a 'third man' trip on a loco footplate with him. We had loco No 1 with the Victorian train, which was another very enjoyable day out.

I was finding that the more time I spent at Tywyn, the more I wanted to get involved and do. Looking back at those two days, although enjoyable in their own right, guarding and loco work were not for me. Being a train guard is a very responsible position that requires a lot of time and training to achieve and I felt that it would be difficult to be able to spend the time there to get the required training. I had soon decided that loco work was a young man's game, having had to be on shed at 7.15am on my day as 'third man'. Climbing all over No 1 to clean it and prepare it for the day was hard work. Again the training required, starting as a cleaner, takes time. I therefore decided to start training as a station assistant, and depending on how that went I would then see what else I could do. I found the hardest part of the training was getting to know all about ticket sales, all the different types and making the figures balance at the end of the day. It is a responsible job, as are all jobs on a public railway, but so enjoyable. You are usually the public's first contact with the railway, so the PR side is very important.

There is never a dull moment at a station with a train in the platform or due and plenty of passengers about. Sorting out problems, answering no end of questions about everything and helping in many ways when required is a wonderful way to spend a day. While training I was with someone different every time and I came to the conclusion that every station master really enjoys the job, meeting so many people every day when on duty.

Having been passed as a station assistant I decided next to try training as a blockman. Although I have only just started training and have a very long way to go I have realised that blocking is great fun, but it is also a very responsible job that must not be taken lightly. I hope one day to be passed as a blockman and look forward to spending peaceful days in a blockpost.

This then is how I became involved with the Talyllyn Railway – but why, who knows? Having had an interest in railways all my life and having visited most of the preserved railways, maybe I saw this as a way of putting something back into railways that have given me so much enjoyment. There is no doubt that once started you become very easily hooked and want more and more. The one thing about other TRPS volunteers you meet on a working weekend or on duty is that, like you, they are there because they want to be. If they did not, they would not do it. Maybe this is the reason why everyone is so friendly and helpful. The TR is not the biggest preserved railway, it is not the richest, it does not carry the highest number of passengers a year, it certainly is not the longest, and nor does it have any great plans about extensions, etc, but it has one thing no other railway can boast. It was the first preserved railway, and if it had failed 60 years ago who can guess what we would have today? Perhaps that is why TRPS volunteers come back time and again to the railway they love. I have one regret about all this, that I did not do it more than 30 years ago when I first discovered the Talyllyn Railway.

Moira Ventry

My husband has been volunteering for several years on the Talyllyn Railway and at the end of February 2010 I agreed to join him on the Outdoor Working Week and become part of the track relaying gang.

As a child one of my favourite activities was mucking in with my Dad on various DIY projects, such as building our garage and an extension to our house. So I knew a bit about mixing concrete and the like. Also my father had spent his working life as a 'P Way man', first in a maintenance gang, then as a supervisor, so I was going to be experiencing a bit of what he had done during his working life.

I left home on the Sunday with a mixture of expectation and apprehension. Expectation because I was looking forward to mucking in with the work and finding out first-hand about the different parts of a relaying job; apprehension because I knew I was not physically fit enough to shovel ballast and didn't know how much of the work I could physically do.

We travelled up on the Sunday and after tea went to the gang briefing, where we were told about the jobs that were being undertaken during the week. As there were not as many people as

Volunteers' stories

Tracklaying at Nant Gwernol, not long before the opening of the extension in May 1976. *TR Collection*

Unloading rail from the company lorry in the early days. *TR Collection*

usual it was decided that only two big jobs should be tackled: the building of a weighbridge building, and some relaying at Brynglas crossing. I was relieved to find that the bulk of the people were in their 60s or 70s and there was a big range of physical fitness.

On Monday the first part of the job at Brynglas was taking the old track out. To begin with I helped to carry the new rails into place: eight people were positioned along the rail in pairs, and we used rail tongs; these clamp over the head of the rail and the weight of the rail holds them in place. The longest rails were 36 feet long and weighed 50lb per yard, so we each lifted 75lb in weight. We lifted the rails onto special trolleys called skates and pushed them along the track to where the relaying site was.

Working in Dolgoch Bottom Woods. *TR Collection*

job, which was to wire-brush all the fishplates that were taken out of the track. It was a nice job because it had started snowing, and I had the excuse that I could sit in the shelter of the station building out of the snow; also, when the fishplates were rubbed down it was something I could say I had done all by myself.

Another job I did was to clear the muck out of the holes in the sleepers. The sleepers were in reasonable condition and we needed to reuse them, so we put a substance called spikefast into the holes. This is supposed to expand and fill the holes, but because the temperature was below freeing the spikefast did not work perfectly and fully expand.

I went home after two days and the gang spent the rest of the week putting the track back in and finishing off the job. I had had a really pleasant two days.

Next we took the old track out. First we took the fastenings out of the track with a special type of crowbar. I was surprised how easy this was. We then took these rails away on the skates, dug out the sleepers and levelled the ballast with pickaxes.

After we took the track out we laid concrete as a foundation for the crossing. First we needed to wait for the local farmer to dig out the bed, then we hand-mixed a concrete base. Later we put in a steel frame to reinforce the concrete, and later in the week, after I had gone home, ready-mixed concrete was poured to form the crossing.

On the second day I was given a special

A track working party with loco No 5 *Midlander*, **Colin Roobottom driving.** *TR Collection*

Volunteers' stories

A glimpse into the future

The continuation of the Talyllyn Railway depends on future generations continuing to volunteer, and it is very fortunate in having a flourishing Young Members Group. From time to time the Group organises a Young Members' Day, when it takes responsibility for the operation of the railway, and all the operating roles, from Controller down, are performed by Young Members.

In 2010, on Young Members' Day, the Group had a display at Wharf station to encourage young visitors to start volunteering. Items from the display are reproduced here as a tribute to the Group and all its hard work; we hope they will encourage other young people to offer their services so that the TR will be running for many years to come.

CLARE EVANS

My association with the Talyllyn started at the age of 7 when my Dad set up the Tracksider group. When I was 14 I was able to start volunteering in the Traffic Department, first as a trainee until you get promoted and move through the grades where I am now a Passed Assistant Guard and Stationmaster.

I also love getting involved in the social events and the working parties that the YMG organise. The YMG makes the Talyllyn experience much more enjoyable for young members as it gives them a close group of friends, making the experience of volunteering so much more sociable.

CHRIS PALMER

Hi, I'm Chris. I have been volunteering on the Railway for 7 years as a Traffic member and many more as a Tracksider. In 2009 I spent 6 amazing months in Tywyn so if you were here then, you have probably already met me! I love meeting new people all the time and the YMG helps to achieve that.

I also stayed in the volunteer hostel (Llechfan); there's a great unity in there, if you need something there is always someone to help out. I hope to see lots more new people volunteering in the future, You won't regret It... But more importantly for now, have a wonderful time when you visit the Talyllyn Railway!! **Chris is now a Passed Assistant Guard.**

KATE WENBORN

Hey! I'm Kate and I have been a volunteer for five years now. I first joined as part of my Duke of Edinburgh, and whilst I was here I made many friends and now keep coming back.

I started off doing both Traffic and Loco work, however found loco was more for me and so continued with it. I also help with working parties throughout the year and assist with repainting things around the Railway.

The reason why I keep coming back is for the people – I have made some amazing friends here who I regularly see away from the Railway. If you are considering joining – do it!

MATT PEAT

I'm Matt and for a few years now I have been volunteering in the Loco department on the Talyllyn Railway, where I am now an experienced Cleaner. My role includes the responsibility of preparing the engines and learning the art of firing. I am also the chairman of the Young Members Group.

In my opinion my experience of volunteering has been enhanced by the activities of the YMG; from sponsorship events to socials on the beach, having a group of friends to spend time with and live with when I come to Tywyn makes the experience so much more enjoyable, and I would love to invite anyone to join us and get involved! You won't regret it!

EMILY SMITH

I'm Emily Smith, aged 18. I have been volunteering on the Talyllyn Railway for 4 years and have loved every minute of it. I mainly get involved in the traffic side of things, I love meeting new people. As well as working on the trains, I am a seasonal member of staff in the railway's cafés.

I never used to enjoy steam trains but meeting people on the railway made me feel wanted and I have now grown to love working there. The YMG has a big impact on my volunteering as we always do activities, have parties and see what we can do to help the railway, such as painting carriages. All these activities bring people on the railway closer, we're all just one big family!!

ROGER BRENT

My name is Roger and I have been volunteering on the Talyllyn for about a year. I work in the traffic department as an Assistant guard, and also do some station work.

The YMG makes volunteering on the railway extremely enjoyable. Everyone is really friendly and I have made many good friends.

Staying in Llechfan is good fun (and dirt cheap !) and there is often a group of people to be found in the lounge relaxing in the evenings.

Roger is now a passed Assistant Guard.

RICHARD COTTON

My name is Richard and I have been volunteering on the Talyllyn ever since I was a young boy. I started out as a Tracksider; but these days I work in the Traffic Department as an Assistant Guard.

I also love getting involved with the working parties and I think that this is the best thing that the YMG contributes to the Talyllyn Railway.

For me the YMG makes the whole Talyllyn experience so much more enjoyable for young people, as they have an identity and a strong group of friends which makes volunteering, and living in the hostel Llechfan so much more sociable.

2 Volunteers' photo gallery

TALYLLYN preservation 60 1951 - 2011

Right: **Guard Alistair McDonald walks back along his down train at Dolgoch Falls station in the early days of the TR** The lady standing by the seat is in traditional Welsh costume; Sue Whitehouse identifies her as 'Mrs Hannah Evans, who used to appear often in Welsh costume on the railway'. *TR Collection*

Below: **Platform Inspector Alan Doe (left) and Duty Controller Nigel Adams pose on a sunny day at Wharf station.** *Nigel Adams collection*

In August 1989 a young cleaner polishes up loco No 6 *Douglas* in Pendre loco shed before it leaves to collect its carriages from the carriage shed to go to Wharf station for its passengers. *R. J. Morland*

Colin Roobottom in Pendre Works. *TR Collection*

Volunteers' photo gallery

The late David Ratcliff on No 2 *Dolgoch* (minus its nameplates) pulls the empty stock from the North Carriage Shed at the start of a glorious day in 1986. *R. J. Morland*

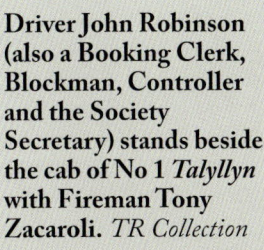

Driver John Robinson (also a Booking Clerk, Blockman, Controller and the Society Secretary) stands beside the cab of No 1 *Talyllyn* with Fireman Tony Zacaroli. *TR Collection*

The late Phil Guest looks back along his down train as he brings it into Rhydyronen. The loco is No 3 *Sir Haydn*.
TR Collection

Station Master Ivor Moody talks to Driver Chris Parrott as No 1 *Talyllyn* is watered at Abergynolwyn. This is not a regular event as locos normally water at Dolgoch, but the facility is there if needed. *TR Collection*

Volunteers' photo gallery

Driver Terry Gurd (on the fireman's side of *Talyllyn*) finds something to smile about as the photographer takes the photo with Guard Peter Briggs giving the 'right away' to a train at Abergynolwyn. *TR Collection*

No 2 *Dolgoch*, with an Engineering train, passes No 1 *Talyllyn* in the siding at Abergynolwyn. *TR Collection*

Abergynolwyn station is licensed for civil wedding ceremonies. During the wedding the special train for the wedding party and their guests sits in the West platform or in the loop, depending on the timetable in force on the day. On 27 May 2001 the loco crew of the wedding special are Chris Price (Fireman), Mike Green (Driver) and John Bilsbury (Cleaner/third man).
R. J. Morland

The end of the day! Driver Jonathan Mann and Fireman Peter Kent Mason are the crew of No 2 *Dolgoch* in Pendre Yard on 3 August 2001.
R. J. Morland

Volunteers' photo gallery

Gerry Young at Quarry Siding blockpost.

Driver Charlie Daniel brings his down train into Abergynolwyn, passing the blockpost and the Blockman, Philip Sayers. *TR Collection*

Steve Griffiths and Noel Williams take it easy at Dolgoch station. *TR Collection*

'Danger – men at work!' The late Graham Jenkins (who died tragically young at 33), Ian James, Steve Griffiths and Colin Hope unload rail. *TR Collection*

Volunteers' photo gallery

During a photographic special on a wet March day, Guard Nigel Adams watches as Fireman Alex Eyres waters No 1 *Talyllyn* at Dolgoch, using the wooden chute and the old water tower. The photographers are travelling in the uncoupled bogie brake-van in the distance, as the train is made up of slate wagons and Van 5. *Chris Worley*

Phil Higginson waters No 2 *Dolgoch* at Dolgoch station, also using the old water tower and the wooden chute, also for the benefit of a photographic special. This always attracts a lot of interest from passengers when it is done. *TR Collection*

Volunteers' photo gallery

Encourage the youngsters! Guard Justin Adams stands alongside his nephew Jesse in the doorway of the brake-van in May 2004. By letting children have pictures like this taken on the brake-van and the loco, the railway hopes to encourage their future participation. *Celia Adams*

The TR 'family' is part of the job. The late Janet Cox (Duty Controller) and Nigel Adams (Platform Inspector) are seen with Richard and Edmund Brown. Richard subsequently volunteered for some years but now has a family of his own. Parents Malcolm and Angela are long-standing TRPS members and Malcolm is a driver; the children are waiting for him to bring his train into Wharf. *Nigel Adams collection*

3 Landmarks and events

TALYLLYN preservation 60 1951 - 2011

Extracts from the 1955 Talyllyn Railway Official Guide – how times have changed!

JOIN THE TALYLLYN RAILWAY PRESERVATION SOCIETY.

Your journey over this unique and historic railway has only been made possible by the efforts of this Society. If you have enjoyed it, will you record your appreciation by completing the form on the last page of this booklet and handing it, with your subscription, to the staff in charge at the Wharf station office on your return? Or you may post it direct to the address given on the form.

When the Society took over the Talyllyn Railway in 1951 the permanent way was in such a deplorable state that it was very doubtful whether a service could be maintained at all. Since then great improvements have been made but an immense amount has still to be done. Permanent way relaying is extremely costly both in labour and materials and this work continues to be the heaviest liability which the Society has to face. If your journey has not been as smooth as you would wish, the remedy lies in your hands. In order that others may enjoy their journeys over this historic railway in the years to come, will you help the good work by joining the Society now? Your subscription will help to buy rails, spikes and sleepers and your hands can help to lay them.

The minimum annual subscription of £1 (One Pound) will entitle you to free travel on the railway, to receive the Reports on progress which the Society issues from time to time, and to attend the meetings of the Society. Life membership costs £15.

Landmarks and events

A special evening train about to leave The Wharf.

No. 4 "Edward Thomas" and train about to leave Brynglas.

Loco No 3 *Sir Haydn* is seen after its rebuild in 1968. This was the first rebuild to be wholly carried out in Pendre Works.
TR Collection

Landmarks and events

A train at Abergynolwyn in the early days. It appears that preparatory work has been started for the installation of the Tea Van siding. *TR Collection*

No 2 *Dolgoch* is at Abergynolwyn in the early days of operation. *TR Collection*

By 1968 Abergynolwyn station has been demolished for rebuilding, although the Tea Van siding is still in place. *TR Collection*

In 1969 No 3 *Sir Haydn* stands at Abergynolwyn with a passenger train during the rebuilding of the station. *TR Collection*

Landmarks and events

The project

The Talyllyn Railway is being extended for a further ¾ mile to a new terminus at Nant Gwernol. The extension will give passengers access to an area of outstanding natural beauty high up above the Nant Gwernol ravine and will open up dramatic views of the Dysinni Valley to passengers on the trains. Footpaths are to be cut back from Nant Gwernol to Abergynolwyn and the station. The work is being carried out by volunteer effort and is scheduled for completion by 1975. It involves the clearance of more than 20 years undergrowth; widening the track base, including blasting out some areas of rock; removing 3 000 yd³ of spoil; placing 300 yd³ of fill; building 9 culverts and small bridges; building a forest road access crossing; laying 1 400 sleepers; 7 800 ft of rail and 600 ton of ballast; running 1 300 yd of telephone cable; erecting 1 800 yd of fencing; cutting footpaths and building a station. It is estimated that the work will require 60 000 volunteer man hours and cost approximately £17 000.

The Wales Tourist Board has awarded the Railway a grant of 49% towards the cost of the project in recognition of its value to tourism.

Should you wish to make a donation, we thank you and ask that you to send it direct to Talyllyn Railway, Nant Gwernol Project, c/o Hon. Treasurer, Flat 2, 61 Broad Road, Sale, Cheshire.

The work of constructing the extension is largely being carried out by volunteer effort, ranging from individuals, to Scout troops, school parties etc. together with the members of the Talyllyn Railway Preservation Society, a band of volunteers from all over the world who give up time and money to

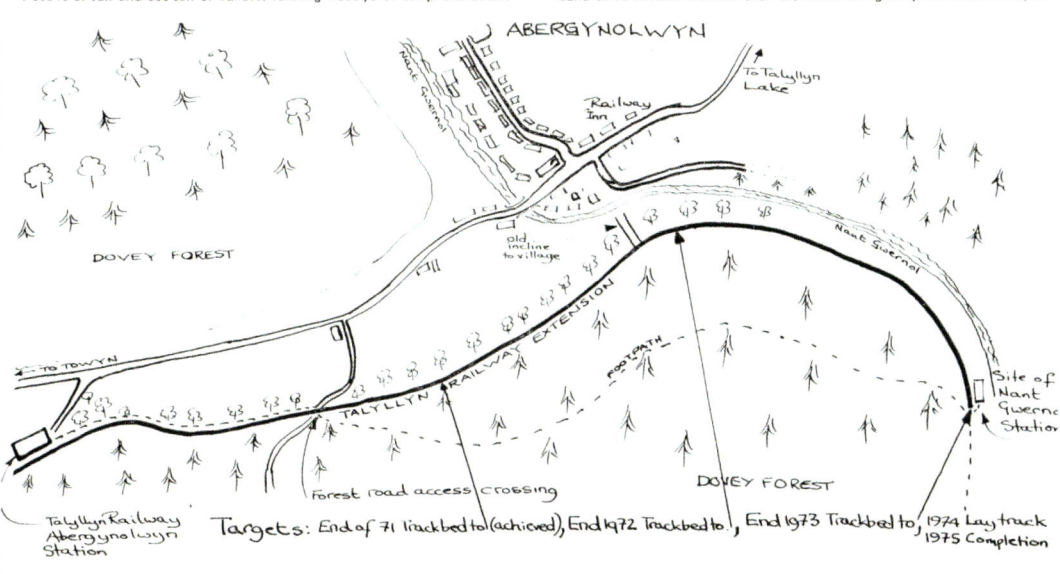

A leaflet appealing for donations to help the Nant Gwernol Project in the mid-1970s.

The first train to run through to Nant Gwernol to mark the opening of the extension in May 1976 is seen here at Abergynolwyn. The Driver was Dai Jones, the Fireman Phil Guest and the Guard Michael Howard. *TR Collection*

A superb shot of No 1 *Talyllyn* and two slate wagons at Nant Gwernol. *D. J. Mitchell*

Landmarks and events

On 6 May 1991 loco No 7 was named *Tom Rolt* at Abergynolwyn by Tom's widow Sonia. Watched by TV and film crews, Driver Mike Green gives the nameplate a final polish before the naming ceremony. *TR Collection*

The late Peter Bold, with Richard Hope, Sonia Rolt and Jeremy Wilkinson, stands in front of the loco, its name still covered by the Welsh flag. Driver Mike Green is on the footplate. *TR Collection*

Two views of the 'Corris Tattoo Special' at Abergynolwyn, circa 1992. 'Tattoo' was the maker's class name of the loco (No 4), and this was the first time it was painted in the Corris Railway livery. It was later painted red and reverted to being *Peter Sam*. *TR Collection*

Landmarks and events

These two photographs were taken at the launch of *Peter Sam* in April 1993. Rev Wilbert Awdry is in the centre of the first picture, and in the second waves the train off from Abergynolwyn with the green flag. *TR Collection*

Loco No 4 carried the name *Peter Sam* for a number of years, and the TR used to have 'Peter Sam's Birthday' events. During one such occasion Duty Controller Nigel Adams (left) stands by the loco with the 'Thin Controller', Tony Thorpe. *Nigel Adams collection*

The late David Ratcliff and Fireman (now Driver) Keith Foster are the crew on *Peter Sam*. David was, and Keith is, a superb railway modeller. *TR Collection*

Landmarks and events

Driver Dai Jones and Fireman David Jones stand in front of No 6 *Douglas* with Anne Owen and Daniel Owen on the occasion of the Hugh Jones Memorial Train, during the September 1995 Society AGM. *TR Collection*

Steve Griffiths and Andy Fox work at Wharf station on 29 August 2003, preparing the ground for the temporary cafe building to be relocated from the end of Wharf station platform to this location on the opposite side of the line. This was to allow the work to commence for the new station and Narrow Gauge Railway Museum. *TR Collection*

Wharf station transformed with its smart new buildings. *TR Collection*

Part of the Narrow Gauge Railway Museum concentrates on signal boxes and signalling equipment. *TR Collection*

Landmarks and events

On 13 July 2006 the newly extended Wharf station and Narrow Gauge Railway Museum was opened by HRH Prince Charles. Here he unveils the plaque to mark the occasion. Also pictured are HRH The Duchess of Cornwall and Keith Theobald, who was at that time the Chairman of the TRPS Council. *TR Collection*

After the unveiling, Prince Charles and the Duchess of Cornwall went across to meet children from local schools who had enjoyed a grandstand view of the occasion from the other side of the track. *TR Collection*

Above: TRPS President Richard Hope welcoming guests to the 60th anniversary re run of the first train. With him are Lis Mann, TRPS chairman and John Snell who fired the first train in 1951

Left: John Snell, who fired the first train on 14th May 1951, on the footplate of No.2 at Rhydyronen on 14th May 2011. No.2 worked the first train.

Right: In 1951 the carriages were pushed past the engine at Rhydyronen. This is no longer possible as the siding has been removed, so the coaches were pushed at Brynglas. *All David Mitchell*